Peaceful Relationships

Wendy Hill

Tellwell Talent
www.tellwell.ca

ISBN
978-0-2288-3014-6 (Hardcover)
978-0-2288-3012-2 (Paperback)
978-0-2288-3013-9 (eBook)

Foreword

THIS BOOK IS DEDICATED TO my late mother Vera, who had many difficulties in her life and still chose to be a loving, kind, and peaceful lady. She tried on a daily basis to be an example of a kind and peaceful human being. I'd also like to acknowledge my siblings for being loving and kind to me and giving me a great childhood memories. Lastly I want to acknowledge my daughters Brandy, Kiana and Kaylee, who have shown me how much love we can have in relationships, even with such unique personalities, I love them all dearly. My grandchildren are my precious family members who are such a blessing to me and their loving relationship is irreplaceable.

Introduction

AFTER I WROTE MY FIRST book, *Understanding Life... What My Ancestors Taught Me Through My Dreams*, I was very relieved to be done with it and satisfied that I had listened to the spirit world. About a month into my freedom of not thinking about this big responsibility of writing and completing this, I had another dream. In the dream, my guide came to me and told me how happy and proud of me they (the spirit world) were with me listening to them. I wrote my first book not because I like to write; I wrote because they asked me to write the teachings that they gave to me through my dreams. Then they said, *We want you to start the second one, and we want you to write about how to have peaceful relationships.*

I was very upset because it took me ten years to write the first one, and it pestered me every time I wasn't writing. It was like that high school or college assignment that you need to get done, but instead you're having fun. So now I was told I had to write another one, and she explained why. They told me it was the inability to have peaceful relationships with others and self that is the root cause of addictions, mental illnesses, and violence. They said if people knew how to have peaceful relationships and to be at peace in their life, they could be healthy.

Many people weren't taught how to be at peace with life but instead were angry with how their lives had unfolded. Being angry when things go wrong is the normal for many people. Experiencing so much trauma and abuse can cause much anger and fear. This was very present in the past generations, as well as today. Our parents are our first teachers about many things, and many parents, grandparents, and great-grandparents have been through many horrific events. I know my ancestors were; they were hunted just because they existed. The colonizers wanted to rid this land of any Indigenous people so that they could have this continent for themselves.

I know that many people have a horrific survival story. It's this history that many people are being affected by, causing anger and dissatisfaction with their lives. One time, I was given a short but powerful message while dancing in a sun dance. A spirit came to me while I was dancing and praying to help to stop the war across the ocean. This grandfather spirit said to me, "Every time you open your mouth, ask yourself, 'Am I creating peace or war?'" He told me to make my home peaceful and my family loving and accepting of each other. When I am done getting my family peaceful, I should go to the next family so they can become peaceful and accepting of each other. He said, "When you can get to the people in your community and in your lands, only then can you go across the ocean to try to bring peace to other lands and people." So the message was to start with my own home.

Many times, the understanding of why we had to experience the events in our lives doesn't come to us until later in life, and only if we are open to the lesson. We often end up with negative thoughts about situations and people and feeling like a victim. This thought of being a victim and blaming someone, the government, the church, family, etc., only gives us an avenue to direct our anger or hate; it doesn't help us to live in a peaceful state. This way of thinking keeps us angry and eventually makes us sick. Our bodies are meant to be at peace and calm, not tightened from the anger or stress.

If you reflect on your own life and our relationships, you will know if you're good at relationships, or not, by looking at the ones you have or don't have in your life. Use this as an indicator of your ability to relate to others. We need to ask ourselves, "How much responsibility for these good or bad relationships are because of my behaviour, attitude, etc.?" "How am I contributing to this relationship?" "Would I be a friend to me?" "Am I someone I find interesting or helpful?" These are all helpful questions to ask yourself, and if you don't see anything wrong with yourself, then ask people close to you. Maybe your children, siblings, parents, friends, coworkers — ask them if there is something they could change about you. What should you change? Or to be very direct: "What don't you like about me?" Then stand back and be open to whatever you hear, because you asked. You might want to ask, "Can you tell me in the nicest way possible?" These questions will help you to start to take an honest look at yourself and to transform into the person you want to be.

There are many policies and procedures developed for centuries by the Europeans to divide and conquer, not only Native people, but really everyone. This process of dividing people begins when we start school and we aren't allowed to help our fellow students. Sometimes divisions start sooner, by our parents if they teach us racism, or favouritism of children or grandchildren. In school, if a person was struggling with a question asked by the teacher, and you tried to help them answer, you were probably discouraged and disciplined for it. This starts our unhealthy and uncaring attitude that we develop but are not comfortable with. As we go through life, we get used to the idea that it's every person for themselves, it's a survival race, and there is no room for compassion, love, and caring, or you get in trouble or taken advantage of.

When I think back to my school days, I can remember the students who stood out; they were the ones who felt awkward with others. I believe to this day they felt awkward because it was an unnatural way of being unhelpful toward each other. We are made from love, and we are all about love. What is uncomfortable is the way school and the workforce try to condition us to be uncaring, disconnected, and competitive toward each other. A physical example is within an office space and everyone is separated by those little partitions. This has been the reason we have so much hurt, lack of trust, disconnection, racism, and many dysfunctions. This makes it difficult to have peaceful relationships, not only with ourselves, but also with others who believe different things than us or look different. We have been impacted in many ways to fear each other and to *judge* each other. All these tactics have worked to keep the people divided, but it also can prevent us from having a connection with a higher power, IE., Creator or God. This is the downfall of all these policies and tactics of colonization. Since our spirit is part of the Creator, we also lose a part of ourselves in this way of thinking.

In the times of survival, you needed people; they were seen as an asset, not a burden. This needing each other is what helped our people to learn to get along. It's like that island mentality; it's such a small living space that you will keep running into them, so you might as well deal with the problem rather than trying to ignore it. To be able to deal with problems in a respectful way is how peace can be maintained. There is no use in holding a grudge if you're going to keep running into the person, so learn to forgive.

What is peace? Why is it important to have? How do we get there, and once we get there, how do we maintain it? How do we know when we have it or don't have it? These are all-important questions, and hopefully I will be able to answer these questions. Peace is a powerful force within our spirit. It is an essential need for the spirit within. My teaching about spirit and life is that every living force has a need to have peace. Even though science has tried to understand and explain life through its research processes, many of its techniques have been inhumane when it comes to animals and life forces. This is why it's been difficult to accept all the results, especially when it comes to understanding each other and life. If you look at the image that has been given to nature and the wilderness, most people have an idea or image of nature as dangerous and something to fear. Most people have a fearful image of wild animals, but within the Native teachings we see them as a family member that has a spirit. Because of this spirit, it also has a need to experience peace and love.

The idea of war only comes when being provoked or attacked or, as in nature, it is absolutely necessary. Since non-Natives have come to this land (North America), it seems as if the Europeans have been at war with nature and the animals that live among us. That is why it is so difficult to understand and relate between the two races. We don't see the natural world or each other as an enemy but rather a relative. This understanding and belief is difficult to remove, no matter what is done to our people. So this knowledge is where I come from. I have worked as a traditional healer for over twenty years and have helped many people to come to be at peace with their situations. This ability to be at peace and accept what is happening in our lives is a gift. When we are not at peace, we are not calm within. Instead, we are bothered, addicted, mentally preoccupied, angry, afraid, hateful, frustrated, nervous, paranoid, disappointed, vengeful, and stressed out. This way of life takes a physical toll on us in so many ways. Eventually, we will get sick, whether it is in our mind or in our body. This is because we are not meant to go through life in this negative state, stressed out.

The boarding/residential schools and even private school policies disconnected us from our family first and sent children into survival mode. Many children have had to go to school far away from their parents and families, and they suffered, mentally, emotionally, physically, sexually, and most importantly, spiritually. Even if it is a church-run school or a religious school, every child needs their connection to family or their race. A healthy, loving, nurturing family is what our spirit needs. These people were sent away, or in many Native peoples' stories, they were stolen by a government employee and placed into these institutions.

They weren't given nurturing, loving, secure relationships and environments; instead, they were abused and for many it was so brutal they didn't survive. There were many Native children who ended up in unmarked graves in the yards of these boarding/residential schools. This greatly impacts our beginning with relationships. How can you learn to connect with others when you don't feel safe or loved? What about the parents or the families who believed the government was doing a good deed by feeding and educating their children, but in reality it was a nightmare?

When children are raised surrounded by others that care deeply for each other, they behave differently. Some people who grew up at a residential school told me, "When we grow up with people who will not be in our lives once we're done school, what's the point of connecting? If the people taking care of you are only abusing and hurting you, how can you learn to love? This is the behaviour we learned; this is how we learned to treat people. If you do bond with another person, it will only hurt if you love and care about them, and then they are gone."

The other thoughts shared by survivors of these schools are of anger and hate toward the family/community who sent them to survive in these scary and abusive environments. Almost every race of people has experienced this in their history. Another act of surviving this type of environment is to ignore or suppress those feelings of anger, sadness, loneliness, and hate, because showing those emotions is discouraged. As a child, many are expected only to be happy, loving, cute, and cuddly, because they are small in size, they are vulnerable, and that's a survival skill. The other outcome of leaving family very young is that you don't really bond with anyone, or you find it difficult throughout life. There are many people who were adopted or have been placed in foster care who suffer in this inability to have intimate relationships. When these children experience hurtful and unloving families, again they have difficulties having healthy and meaningful relationships. I also have met children who had loving adopted families but still didn't connect because they knew they weren't their biological family. The family or people that you really want to connect with are not there. Once you grow up without them, you can grow resentful for not having them around to protect you or play with or learn from and be cared for by them.

Peace or Skenoh

S o what is Peace? In our language we say "Skenoh." When we greet one another, we use this term. My ancestors knew how important it is to have peace within, and this knowledge has been passed down. I learned that our first concern is, "Do you have peace/wellness in you?" But I was taught this important lesson, that the root word of this word "Skenoh" comes from the root word of "Skeno:o," which means to go slow. So to have peace within, we must slow ourselves down. We must slow down our thoughts, our actions, or reactions. This is how we can get to having peace. We must pay attention to our thoughts and ask ourselves if these thoughts are good thoughts — if these thoughts are true, and if we are sure that this is a truthful fact. Many times we assume and convince ourselves that we just know. It's these thoughts that are causing us to be upset and angry. When we react quickly and don't think about the consequences and the wanted outcome, we will make many mistakes. These mistakes are what can ruin our relationships. This is where we will start, slowing down our reactions and stopping and thinking things over.

The Peacemaker

My people had a great messenger who came to this area of North America. His name was the Peacemaker, and he brought a great change for our people. Today, we still utilize his message. He was special, kinda like Mahatma Gandhi I love his knowledge and attitude that was shared. One such quote "The weak can never forgive. Forgiveness is the attribute of the strong." There was also another important man regarding peaceful ways or Siddhattha Gotama Buddha, or Gautama Buddha or simply the Buddha, after the title of Buddha. He was a monk, mendicant, sage, a philosopher, teacher and religious leader on whose teachings Buddhism was founded. Here are a few of his quotes; "The mind is everything. What you think you become. When the mind is pure, joy follows like a shadow that never leaves." "All that we are is the result of what we have thought." "Peace comes from within. Do not seek it without." He believed that enlightenment, or Nirvana, was achieved when one's mind is compassionate, free of attachment and focused on the present moment. "The secret of health for both mind and body is not to mourn for the past, nor to worry about the future, but to live the present moment wisely and earnestly." "Every morning we are born again. What we do today is what matters most." "A person is not called wise because they talks and talks again; but if a person is peaceful, loving and fearless then they is in truth called wise." "Remembering a wrong is like carrying a burden on the mind." "Our life is shaped by our mind; we become what we think. Suffering follows an evil thought as the wheels of a cart follow the oxen that draws it." "Holding onto anger is like grasping a hot coal with the intent of throwing it at someone else; you are the one who gets burned." "A generous heart, kind speech, and a life of service and compassion are the things which renew humanity." The peacemaker carried similar teachings and was a perfect example of love, understanding, compassion and caring for others. He was born to a virgin Huron woman, and grew faster than the other boys his age. People thought he was strange because he went off by himself a lot. He didn't let it bother him how they treated him and just learned to play on his own. He taught us how to live with peace within ourselves and how this affects the people around you. He did a great job for the Creator in stopping war and teaching the power of unity and safety through love and caring for each other. He brought awareness about having a positive state of mind, a way of having a disciplined way of thinking. We call it "Ganigohiyoh," or having a good mind.

Another gift he gave to the people was compassion and love. When we care for each other, we create a loving environment. He made a warring people become family-like and to help and care for each other. When we are mean to each other, we don't feel safe, and this causes hurt feelings, and then violent behaviour develops. Abusive behaviour toward others creates abusive people. When we don't feel safe, we cannot have peaceful thoughts. Instead, we become paranoid or afraid of each other, never feeling safe or at peace with others. The safer we feel, the more positive thoughts we have about ourselves, others, our life experiences, and the healthier overall we become. Another message he gave us is to be thankful. When we think about all the things in our lives that are good or right and we acknowledge a higher power, Creator, God, etc. for these gifts we have in our lives, we can instantly feel better. In gratitude we can feel love from above and below our feet, our mother, the earth. This "feeling better" is the positive energy that is created by the positive thoughts, which in turn brings healthiness to our overall well-being. This message he gave is a very important foundation to having healthy, peaceful, and functioning relationships. We call this Gayenesragowa, or the Great message of Peace. His story and the people involved at this important time in our history is a very important reminder of the behaviour that can cause unhealthy relationships.

The Peacemaker's story has lessons for all of us about our judgments and attitudes about children that are born to unwed or single mothers. The message is, "Every child born is here for a great purpose for the Creator, and for everyone around that child to embrace and love them." This boy was very instrumental in changing a warring people and uniting and organizing thousands of people. He brought the first idea of democracy to North America. He did this by talking to people and helping them to change the way they thought about each other and sharing decision-making.

In his life story, he was being guided by a higher power, and he chose to listen and do what the Creator was telling him to, even though many people thought he was crazy. One of the messages he was given was to make a boat from a white boulder. No one at that time had ever seen or heard of a stone boat floating, but this didn't stop him. When he was finished carving it, it floated. That was when he left his people, because they didn't believe in him, but he was also told where he had to start in stopping the war.

This story is very important, because this is how each of us can learn to live our lives. He didn't believe he was less than others because he didn't have a father growing up; instead, he believed he had a purpose. Even though others talked about him and tried to shame him, he didn't listen to their opinion; he listened to his mother and grandmother, who believed in him, and he spent many hours in solitude listening to a higher power. Today, people use many devices to try to avoid solitude or being alone with their own thoughts. We turn on the radio or the TV, computers, phones, etc., anything that can take our minds away from the thoughts that are coming to us. People also choose to use alcohol, drugs, sex, gambling, anything to take their mind off their thoughts. This is what can disconnect us from the higher power and the guidance that is trying to come to us. The relationship with our own spirit and our spirit guides, ancestors, are also disconnected. We must learn to be quiet without distractions to hear those messages. Maybe it may be a long, quiet car ride or a quiet morning with some coffee on the porch. These are subtle ways of allowing the spirit world to help us to come to a peaceful place within.

Treaties

T HERE WERE MANY TREATIES MADE between the Indigenous people of North America and the Europeans, specifically the British, French, and Dutch. These treaties had no deadline, as a matter of fact, as Johnny Cash sang in his song, "As long as the rivers flow, as long as the sun will rise, as long as the grass shall grow." This is exactly what is in our treaties, so these treaties were made to make peace, and these agreements would be forever.

When the Europeans came here to North America, they saw paradise and a heaven on earth with all the greenery. Many saw the opportunity to get rich. This greed that was inside them, the Indigenous peoples didn't understand, because unlike the Europeans, we never saw individualism and only one person prospering. Instead, we were a village-minded or group-thinking people. Our mentality was, "We can all have a great life, and we will all benefit from our actions." If a person is suffering, their suffering will affect all our suffering, so we never wanted anyone to go without and struggle. Our values were held with compassion for each other, caring for each other because we knew that one day we might need help and compassion from someone.

So, from the beginning there was a clash of ideas and interests with our environment. That was what brought the wars between the Native people and the white people in North America. The Europeans had a problem: my ancestors were in the way. The land was inhabited by Native people who loved it. The treaties were made because no one was backing down, and many people were dying. Our ancestors saw treaties as an opportunity to protect the land and people and ensure their safety. However, many treaties were broken by the European people before the ink was dry. My ancestors were not used to people who broke their word, agreements, and treaties. What the Europeans didn't understand was the fact that Native people had been making treaties and agreements long before Europeans came here to North America. My ancestors recorded these agreements through wampum belts. We recorded agreements and historical events through this method. The "One Dish, One Spoon" agreement was made with many neighbouring Native peoples to agree to share the land and animals as if this area was like a dish that we could all eat from. There was a spoon and not a knife, so no one could get cut by the other, and there would be no bloodshed over hunting, fishing, and trapping on the land. To this day, Native people have a deep hurt for the betrayal of these European people. Many European people have no idea what their ancestors agreed upon to live in North America, but as a Native person growing up, I was told by my parents about this important history. These treaties were agreements on how we would treat and think about each other. These agreements are simple, if you are reminded of them often and shown by the behaviour of the adults around you.

There is one I will share as best as I can. It's called the Guswentha or the "Two-Row Wampum." This was one of the first made between the Iroquois and the British (English), French, and Dutch. This treaty was to help the Europeans and Native people to live with respect and have a peaceful coexistence. But from what my father told me, the Native tribes held a meeting long before this agreement or treaty was made. They picked the Iroquois, or the Five Nations (which later became the Six Nations) to speak for all of the Native people in this agreement. This treaty was done, and because my people were not writing people, they made a wampum belt. The two purple beads went horizontally between white wampum beads. Between the two rows of purple beads were three white rows of wampum beads that represented friendship, peace, and respect. The essence of the agreement was that we would see life as a river going down the river together, but parallel. We wouldn't try to steer each other's boat, nor would we intertwine with each other. Instead, we would have friendship, peace, and respect between our peoples. In their ship or vessel, the Europeans would have their own language, religion, and way of governing their people, and in our canoe we also had our own language, religion, and way of governing our people. We agreed to respect and acknowledge each other's vessels and not interfere with each peoples' ways of life. To this day, as Native people we have lived up to those agreements to the Europeans or visitors to this land.

These are only a few of the treaties that demonstrate our ancestors had thought about the relationship we must have to maintain a peaceful existence.

My First Teacher

M Y MOTHER WAS MY FIRST teacher about having peaceful relationships, and she didn't have much formal education, but she was very intelligent and compassionate. When we were growing up, there were ten of us living in a small, thirty- by twenty-foot house. So I know she had to get good at building peace. My root family consisted of me and three older sisters and three older brothers, one younger brother, mom and dad. I remember the way she worked her magic on our arguments, and I always admired her for that. We had a rule of no yelling or fighting; we were instructed to always bring our conflicts to her. We would sit down with her sitting in the middle of us and then explain her process. Only one person could talk at a time, and she could only listen to one person at a time. We would both get to tell our story.

She would instruct, "Be patient and listen while someone is talking, because you will want the other person to listen while you talk. No yelling. We can settle our differences in a calm voice; it's easier to listen to a calm voice. No complaining after our discussion, and if you have something to say, say it when we're all present."

Her way of solving our problems taught me many great lessons about conflict. One main lesson was that it was okay to disagree, and it was valuable to share my thoughts or opinions. I never was told or shown that my opinions or ideas were of no value. So it was interesting to watch some people who believed you had to shout to get your message heard, or that your opinion didn't matter. Everyone's opinion deserves to be considered.

So, I lived my childhood without fighting. I think my best teacher was one of my older sisters. She wanted to be the boss and for me to follow her and do as she wanted. Being the younger sister, I thought I had to listen to her, since that was something my parents had taught us. If anyone was older than you and they told you to behave or to do something, you had to listen and not talk back. Well, I struggled with this idea of not talking back, because I always considered what people said to me, and if I didn't agree, how would they know unless I expressed it?

As I got older, I noticed I was getting taller than her and started to think about why I had to listen to her. She couldn't make me do it. So one day when I was twelve years old, I said "NO!" to her for the first time on one of her commands. Oh my god, she didn't like that answer! I saw it in her face, and I thought, *No, I have to stop this or it will continue.* So I felt stronger the second time, and I said it in a louder and stronger voice: "NO!!" That was it; she jumped on me and tried to fight me. I couldn't believe how light she was, so I threw her off me, and I got her into a headlock (like I saw on TV wrestling) and held her down. She was so mad, like a wild animal, and I was scared to let her go, so I just held her and was trying to calm her down. I guess my voice wasn't what she wanted to hear, because it just made her more mad. So I started to yell to my other older sister, who came into the bedroom and said, "Stop it!!!"

I said, "It's not me. Come get her, she's out of control, not me."

So my other sister got between us and took her out of the room. Then I realized I was physically stronger than her, and I was never going to be bossed around by her again, well, anyone for that matter.

There were many times growing up that I was challenged with doing what was popular or what was right in my heart. I remember when I was eleven years old and in grade six, it seemed as though the other kids thought I was cool. So we hung out, and I guess we were the cool kids. There was a girl who wasn't being treated very nice by many of the other kids. I went home one day and told my mother about it. She asked me how I felt about it, and I said, "I don't like it."

She said, "Well, you can do something about it, or you can allow it. Include her, and if the rest don't agree, then you choose who you would rather hang with."

So I followed her advice, and the next day I invited the girl to come hang out with the cool kids. Some of the other kids resisted and tried to discourage me, but I said, "No, I want to include her." Somehow, they just listened. For the rest of the school year, she was included in our recess discussions and playing in the playground. She has remained my friend to this day.

Another time in high school, I had a cousin who started dating a young woman in my community. I wasn't one to interfere in other people's relationships, but one day a friend of mine approached me and said, "You need to talk to your cousin and stop him from going out with her. She is my relative and she is a party girl."

Our family was very close growing up, and one of my teachings about family is to look out for their best interests and support each other. So my cousin didn't drink alcohol; many of my relatives didn't. So I told him what her relative told me, and he broke up with her. Well, she didn't take that too well, and she wanted to fight me, so I was scared to go places. I stopped going to hockey games and lacrosse games, then I thought, *No, I'm not going to let this control me.* I was allowing fear to control me. I thought, *I will go wherever I want to go. I won't be controlled by this. I will deal with it.* So the very first hockey game I went to, she was there and confronted me. I told her that I had told him, and it was because I didn't want him to go down that road of alcohol. She was still upset and wanted to fight me. Being the negotiator that I am, I told her, "I don't want to fight you. You go your way, and I will go my way, and if we meet somewhere we will go in opposite directions. I'm not going to fight you." She agreed to this, and from that day on we both lived up to the agreement. Through these experiences, I was learning that there is a choice or alternative behaviour when we are in a conflict. We can choose to talk about the problem and try to come to a solution that we can both live with, or we can make war and fight.

There was another situation that stands out that showed me I had a skill to resolve conflict in a healthy way. Or I guess a better way to say it is that I don't like violence. I was with my little girl at a swimming centre, and we were in the change room getting ready to leave. All of a sudden I heard banging and yelling and crying. I was startled, so I followed the noise. What I came upon was three teenagers beating up another female teenager. I was very upset, and these young women were as big as me — not that I'm very big, but something inside me came forward. The next thing I knew, I hit the side of the locker, which made a big bang, and the girls stopped and looked at me. I said in my loudest, scariest voice, "Stop and get away from her!"

They all stopped and looked at me with big eyes, then one of the young, tough, women said, "Mind your own business, lady, before we hurt you."

I walked right up to her and pulled her hand away from the other girl's collar, and I stared into the bully's eyes and said, "You're not going to do anything to me or her," and I shoved her away from us and put the young beaten woman behind me. Then I said, "I need your names and your phone numbers, and maybe I should have a talk with all your mothers and see how they feel about their daughters being bullies, and I should tell them what I witnessed. Maybe my new friend [the girl hiding behind me] here needs me to be her witness for this assault on her when we call the police to have everyone charged. Or maybe you should leave and never touch her again, because if she ever wants to charge any of you, I'm giving her my number, and she can call me anytime to be her witness of today's events."

Well, needless to say, they all left in a hurry, and I told the young beaten woman, "Make sure you tell your mother what happened, and here is my number." She thanked me and cried and hugged. This event has stayed with me all these years, and it happened almost thirty years ago. I'm only 5'2" and 130 pounds, but I never thought of my size as a handicap; my strength came from something inside me. When your spirit is strong, you can do many powerful things that the physical part might seem incapable of. This belief inside of me to be a protector of "caring, respect, and kindness" was strong. There was a time in my youth when I was affected by meanness, and I tried this behaviour, almost like trying on clothes, but it wasn't for me. It didn't fit me, so I left it behind.

So as I was growing up and having different experiences, I was becoming more aware of the ability to resolve conflict. Another experience that impacted me was when my people were defending our land. There was an occupation on a hundred-acre parcel of land that was to be developed for housing. We were into the battle for over six months of occupation, and there was high tension on both sides of the conflict. The Ontario Provincial Police was trying to get our people off that land using different intimidation techniques. It began in February, and many incidents happened like police raids, beating of our elders, youths, and other people, arrests, racism, confrontations between the local townspeople and Native people. Needless to say, emotions were high and the conflict was dangerous. Well, because of this high tension and the anger and distrust of the police force, they were not allowed on my peoples' territory, the Six Nations of the Grand River.

On one particular day, there was an incident where a police cruiser was observed stopped at a four-way stop in our community. It sat at that stop sign for a few minutes. There was a restaurant kitty-corner from where the car was stopped. The Native people who were sitting at the place saw the OPP car stopped for some time. This group surrounded the car and started to confront the officers about being on our territory (they weren't allowed because of the police raid). Shortly, the car was surrounded, and the people became angry and aggressive. My cousin who was at the reclamation site was sent a text message to go to the police car and stop the attack. He grabbed me to go with him to deal with the incident. I didn't want to go, but he insisted.

So we went there, and it was ugly. The car was surrounded by thirty or so angry people. Some were punching the car's hood, and one of the young men, who was approximately 6'4" and weighed 350 pounds, was lifting up the car by the rear bumper. The officers inside were freaking out, the female officer was crying hysterically, and tensions were high. As I walked closer to this incident, it seemed like something was pulling me into the middle. I really didn't want anything to do with it, but something was telling me to stop it and get those people out of there, or something very harmful was going to happen to us all. I went closer and closer and knew I had to do something right away. I went into the middle of the crowd, hit the police car's hood, and said in my loudest voice, "Stop right now! What do you think you're doing here? This is not your car, and no one has a right to be doing anything to it. Step away from it!"

And to my surprise, they listened, except for the exceptionally large man holding up the back of the car by the bumper. So I looked at him and said, "Put the car down and step away."

He did so, then I continued to talk to the people. "Everyone take a breath. Breathe, you're upset, I can see that, but no one is getting hurt here. This car is leaving our community, and those people are not getting hurt. This is not who we are!!!"

They listened, and we were able to get the car out of that situation without anybody getting hurt. My cousin still laughs about it and says, "Only you can talk hostile people into stopping and taking a breath in the middle of the chaos."

So these are some of the life experiences that have taught me about a basic need inside each of us, the need for peace inside all of us. We would all like to have peace, but we don't always know how to get there, especially when we feel it may be impossible to achieve without losing something. This is the cause of many breakdowns of relationships, not being able to have peace when you're around certain people. Whether it's about race, gender, religion, loudness, age, or whatever might be the reason you don't like them. Maybe they've done something to you in the past that you can't forgive, and therefore you can't have peace in your mind whenever you think about them.

Conflict

I N ORDER TO UNDERSTAND PEACE, you must first understand conflict. In many situations, we try so hard to avoid conflict, but at many costs. Conflict is natural and inevitable in life situations, and there is always going to be a difference of opinions. There are no two people who think exactly alike and have the same values, goals, and ways of going through life — even siblings!

We are all different, and when we can accept that we are different and it's okay and normal, we will have peace. It's okay to have conflicts, but it's nice knowing that it's normal and we can discuss it without having high emotions. Many people don't like conflict and do everything to avoid it because of past events when conflict has led to violence or a scary experience. Avoiding conflict is like trying to avoid breathing; it's going to happen, and we need to accept it and decide how we will deal with it. Many people who have had a negative experience will become afraid of conflict and want to avoid it. When it has occurred in a person's childhood and it was scary, it is even more traumatic. It can be a trigger to expect a very scary experience all over again. Conflict can be an opportunity to discuss the different opinions in a situation. It can be the first time that you will hear a person's strong passion on a topic. It can be a relief for a person to be able to express their strong desires.

Sometimes people can be very strong with their opinions, and their personalities can be disturbing to others. There can be conflict when people differ in religious beliefs and values. It's a very complicated issue because conflict has many layers beneath the strong, passionate expressions. When the conflict and passion is so strong it may go beyond words, it might become a physical expression. Some physical conflicts can be a shove or an actual fistfight. That is why many people don't like conflict, so even when we don't agree with a decision, we won't speak up. That is when we need to ask ourselves, "Is it safe for me to express my disagreement? Is this conversation worth my energy to discuss this further? How important is this to me?"

There are many scenarios you may find yourself in when it comes to conflict. Acceptance is the best way to deal with conflict, knowing that it will happen. It's knowing that you can choose to stay in the conversation and express your thoughts and opinions but also be willing to hear another person's concerns and opinions. It's a way of getting to know another person's passion, and it can be a learning curve. As a boss of a company, it can be a time to hear some concerns from staff. As a parent it may be the first time you actually hear about the issues between siblings. So we can look at conflict as an exciting time to hear some deep concerns or beliefs and opinions. Sometimes we learn to become deaf to people who seem to speak at a higher volume, especially with couples, or parents to children, or teenagers to parents. We don't understand that the reasons we raise our voices are because we are scared that we won't be heard. We might also be afraid that the person is going to make a big mistake, and we care so much for them that we start to raise our voices.

One time, a woman was screaming at her children in front of many people, and I intervened to ask, "Lady, what are you so afraid of? What are you angry about?"

She was so in the habit of speaking in that tone and reacting that way to her children that she said, "Why do you think that?"

I said, "Well, you're raising your voice so much that it's involved all of us within a forty-foot circle."

She shouted, "I'm not mad!!!! I will yell when I am mad!!!"

Her face was beet-red, and her hair was a bit messed up by this point and very scary-looking. I said, "You are yelling and frankly looking really scary, and I'm a grown woman. I can't imagine what your children must think when you act like this."

She just looked shocked and said, "Really?" She became embarrassed and thoughtful.

I said, "I know you must be very passionate about how your children act and your values, but they're probably more concerned with their fear than actually listening to you. If you calm down some and use a more calming tone, they will feel more comfortable listening to you."

She followed me around for a few hours, asking lots of questions about how to change her relationship with her children. She had three teenage daughters, and they were having a very rocky relationship. Her daughters thanked me later that evening. She invited me over for dinner with her family; I know she wanted to be more calm and peaceful to them. I met her husband, and he seemed so relieved there was a person his wife would listen to. There was some definite intervention from a higher power. I was at the right place at the right time.

We stayed in touch for a few years and then lost touch, but I can say I'm happy to have brought relief to her and her family. She was ready to change how she interacted with them as well. I am a firm believer that I can't change or help anyone to change unless they want to change. A human being is very strong in their determination. If they want to stay the same and they believe they are right in their attitude and behaviour, then LIFE consequences will have to be their teacher. Finding peace within also needs faith, coincidences, serendipity, and accidents. If you want to feel at peace with life, you will need to believe there is a plan for us. We do have someone who is watching over us and planning out our lessons for the day. I went to school to be a teacher, and we had to learn to do daily lesson plans, weekly planning, and monthly planning. As we go through life, we have a higher power as well as our spirit guide who does the same for us. Based on our own thoughts, attitudes, and behaviours, and when we are willing to look at ourselves and accept these lessons, we will start to become secure in our destiny.

Sometimes we become so accustomed to treating the people we are supposed to love and be the most loving and supportive of badly, the very people who tear them apart with our words or silence or actions. This happens because we are creatures of habit, and we have reactions that come from our own frustrations and also from behaviour from our families. It's the fear in us that causes many of our scary behaviours with our family. I'm not making excuses for this behaviour; I'm explaining why we yell and overreact to our children or the people closest to us. It's because our emotions are so invested in these relationships that our love, hopes, dreams, and wishes for our children might become too attached to ourselves. We sometimes become so controlling that we push our hopes and dreams onto them, and when it becomes threatened, we react with fear. We must learn to understand fear, and all the behaviour that comes from it, to understand love. These two are opposites. It's a strange relationship that they have within us. Fear can make us act in crazy and scary ways to the ones that we are supposed to love and care for. You can see this on the news everyday: a person who is in love with someone kills them. Why? It's because of the fear of losing them or losing control of them.

Many unhealthy relationships are controlled by fear, the fear of losing the person, fear of the loss of respect. We interpret the behaviour of others as disrespect toward ourselves, and then our EGO starts to take over. The ego is a voice inside of us that says, "Are you going to let them disrespect you like this?" Or "Are you going to let them disrespect our family like this?" Then the violence starts, but the reality is, "Who are we to decide for another human being what they should do with their life?"

I know as parents we are somewhat responsible for guiding our children, but when we are beating or killing them to control them, something is definitely wrong with this. Our children's abilities, destiny, and futures are thoughts inside themselves. It takes a lot of faith to allow the higher power to also guide our children, not just our will and want for them.

The Teachers From the Inside

RELATIONSHIPS ARE A VERY COMMON problem for many people. I want to share a story from my life of a situation that taught me a lesson about relationships. I worked in a women's federal prison as a Native inmate liaison worker. I was there to provide Native spirituality and counselling to the Native women incarcerated there. One day while I was there, a woman was in the isolation unit again, for the hundredth time since I started working there. One of the correctional workers informed me she had tried to commit suicide, so they asked me to go talk to her. I had thought about this woman and our sessions throughout the year. This time I was not going to let her off so easily with her tough and cold attitude. I wanted to hear her true feelings.

I went into her cell. Everything had been taken away that was harmful to her, and all she had was a mattress on the floor. I asked in a very concerned voice, "What are you doing to yourself? You're always getting into trouble and ending up in here. Your arms are all cut up and scarred. You could be doing so much more with your life than sitting inside this little space and harming yourself."

She answered first in an angry voice, "What do you care?"

I said, "Well, I see a lot of potential in you and don't understand why you don't see it and why you're not trying to get an education or something for yourself for when you get out."

She sat there with her head hanging low and said in a trembling voice, "I don't like myself, and I'm sure others don't like me either. I'm just not good with relationships. I don't like to be around other people because of that. I don't ever feel safe, with no one."

I thought for a moment, and then I said, "Do you want to change that? If it's relationships that you struggle with, I can help you. Do you want to learn how to have better relationships with yourself and others?"

She started crying at this point, shaking her head for yes.

I continued, "You know you're always in a relationship. Even when you're inside this room with only yourself, you're still in a relationship with yourself."

Her reply was, "I hate myself, and I can't change that."

My heart sank, and I realized she had no love for herself; therefore, how could she possibly have any love for others? There was no real outside conflict; it was an interior conflict. She had feelings of hopelessness and helplessness in her own thoughts, feelings, and actions, like she had a bully within herself. I told her, "I can help you if you want, but you have to be honest with me, the way you are being right now."

She agreed, and I hugged her and told her, "There is hope, and you can do anything you set your mind to, but you have to really want this and be willing to listen and try new ways of thinking and acting toward yourself and others."

She agreed again, and from that day on, we had many emotional and honest visits. This is the only way to make change for yourself, being honest with yourself and others.

I began from there to teach her about having a better relationship with herself and to care for herself instead of trying to harm herself. Over the months that I spent with her, she began to make changes in the way she thought about herself and others. I taught her to focus on what was right with her, and even it was the tiniest behaviour or fact about herself, to acknowledge it and give thanks for it. For instance, if she were able to see in the morning as she awoke, she should give thanks to the Creator for the gift of sight, or hearing, and so on. If she demonstrated patience, tolerance, care, and understanding, she should acknowledge this and thank herself for that behaviour; that takes self-control, self-respect, and self-discipline. She started to care for herself, and you could see it physically; she was clean more often, her hair was brushed and fixed nice. Emotionally, she started to see her past in a different light as lessons and teaching tools instead of anger and punishment. She learned each day she could be different; she could be better than yesterday. Her greatest achievement was learning to forgive people who hurt her or disappointed her in her past.

Eventually, she started to like herself, and gradually she was able to spend more time out of isolation and in the rest of population. This was a first experience of her actually feeling proud of herself and caring about her whole self. She started to exercise, take courses to get her grade 12, come for her counselling sessions, and have a daily conversation with the Creator. Sometimes she still struggled in one area of her life, but she would get back on track and look at her thinking, feelings, and spiritual and physical needs. I taught her to look at these four parts of herself and see if she was tending to all her needs holistically. If we live in balance, tending to all four parts of ourselves, then we should feel healthy and happy. When you don't know what it means to take care of yourself holistically, how can you be well and happy? We must take an honest look at our four bodies: mental, emotional, physical, and spiritual, to achieve health and well-being.

From that day of our first honest conversation to one year later, she started her weekend visits on the outside. I had tried to help this woman for two years, and she would only tell me lies or what she wanted me to hear. She acted like she was tough and had it together and didn't need any help, like so many people outside the prison walls. She wanted to feel capable of taking care of herself because no one wants to seem helpless or weaker than anyone else, especially not inside a prison. This is what every healthy human being wants, to be able to help yourself, not be dependent on others for your needs. However, the Creator made life so that we would need each other, so we have to learn how to have healthy relationships with everyone.

This woman had been in and out of institutions since she was fifteen because she wasn't good with relationships. I don't want to blame anyone, but she wasn't given very many healthy people in her life to learn from. No one had ever taught her how to have a healthy or good relationship. She was eventually released from prison and carried the attitude that she was going to be better to herself. Now that she had the freedom to treat herself to whatever she wanted to experience, it was going to be healthy and good. This was one of my first great experiences over the years that made me realize that many people just don't know how to have a healthy relationship with themselves and others. Our spirit has a need to be at peace with family, Creator, community, and our ancestors, as well as our past and ourselves.

Relationships: Teachings From an Elder

THIS IS A TEACHING REGARDING relationships that was taught to me a long time ago. An elder explained this teaching about relationships and stages of life by using his hand. He explained to me that in order for a person to become a leader, they must first master relationships. This must know how to have peaceful relationships, and as mothers, grandmothers, fathers, and grandfathers, aunties, and uncles, we are the leaders within families.

I will try to explain as best as I can from this conversation. This is what he explained.

THE THUMB: Represents you, the nail, or the top part of our thumb, represents our mother. Her job is to provide the nurturing, softness, and gentleness. When we look at what being nurturing looks like or feels like, for some it might mean cooking or bathing or just providing the bare essentials for our children, while other people's ideas of nurturing can be to be very kind and caring in many forms. The problem for many is that there is no formal education within the school systems for learning to be good, nurturing mothers or fathers. I know today the education system tries by sending home electronic babies, but it is still not as productive in producing nurturing mothers and fathers.

The question is why is there a need to instruct this when our parents are our first teachers? It is because many people have lost the ability to parent with healthy behaviour, attitude, and emotions. The results of the private or residential/boarding schools were that these institutions produced disconnected, mean, hurt, and scared people. We can see how this has produced unhealthy, angry people and angry, abusive parents. Hurt plus fear equals anger; this is what has happened from this experience. Many Native people have been affected by this experience of the children being stolen or placed in these scary, unhealthy institutions. It can be almost impossible to have love and kindness in our lives as children from these people. This love and kindness is one of the basic needs of the spirit to be able to be healthy and grow. So as mothers, we need to be aware of the great responsibility that the Creator has given us. Since the gift of life was given to women, we were also given responsibility to provide the spiritual needs of our children. We need to have healthy attitudes and behaviour for our children to learn from. Our spirituality is a great help to guiding us with peaceful thoughts and actions.

It is our belief that we all have a spirit within, and this spirit belongs to the same higher power. When we have this universal belief of being connected in that way, we have a caring and love for each other. It is only when we don't believe we are from the same Creator that we can make war. Many wars are created based on the ideas that other people are made from something evil. When we display healthy behaviour and healthy attitudes regarding ourselves and others, we teach this to others. Even today, most of us go to school at the age of four or five, and this is when the ability to have a free, natural conversation stops. Once we start school, we learn an unnatural way to communicate. We must ask for permission, and to speak is frowned upon. Someone once told me they got all the way through high school without ever having to speak. So in this environment we can't really have a relationship with others when we can't communicate. Being able to share what is going on you on the inside, meaning your thoughts, emotions, beliefs, knowledge, wishes, desires, fears, etc. — how can we share them?

The bottom part of our thumb represents our father. His job is to provide support, whether financially or to provide food and shelter. Again, based on how young boys and men are taught by each other, it can be a very difficult life. This is what has caused so much anger and violence in men. The lack of kindness, gentleness, and compassion in boys and young men's lives has a great influence on the kind of man they will become. It's the hurt plus fear instilled in these small children that can stir many negative feelings and thoughts. The difficult part to being male is that the treatment and beliefs for boys and men to be tough. Have a tough exterior, and you won't be picked on. The male species is more about the physical; therefore, they are more violent toward each other. There are so much pressures society places on the boys and men to be protective, supportive, providing leaders, and yet they're groomed not to show emotion. This is not an easy task for any human being. We all have emotions and we all feel, and when a male or female is not allowed to show these emotions, we are creating unhealthy human beings. Emotions are the strength of women, so it is therefore our responsibility to help change this societal pressure.

If a boy or man is too emotional, people think he is gay or abnormal. This is how far we have gone with unhealthy standards of creating unhealthy or unbalanced men. We must help the boys and men to be accepted and welcomed with all their emotions and free to express them. We no longer require tough, disconnected men; we maybe need them physically strong, with a connection to their feelings. To be at peace with our father, we must accept him as he is, whether he was a healthy and present father or not. My father was pretty stubborn, and he could be difficult to talk to because of how set he was in his ways. I learned to accept him as he was and to be able to have a peaceful and loving relationship with him, it would have to be me that needed to accept him, and I actually admired him for the stance that he took on most subjects. It's not that I always agreed with his opinion; I realized that that was who he truly was, and life made him that way. If I wanted to be able to know him, I had to see that he was showing me a part of himself, and I could just be happy that I had a father and he was present in my life. It was I that I could change and accept in order to have a peaceful relationship with him.

Together they make up you, and to be able to love yourself, you need to be able to love your parents, because that is what makes you up. I realize some parents were just so horrible to their children that it's a very difficult thing to do, and that's understandable, but if you can say to yourself, "I love them but I don't like the choices they made or make, because they brought me into this world to let me experience life." It is our thoughts that affect how we feel, and if we have positive, loving thoughts, we will produce positive feelings, which brings good health. We can't change our past and childhood, but we must accept it to be at peace with it.

So with all the single mothers or single fathers who are raising children, we need to be aware of how we speak about the absent parents. My mother taught me as I was raising my daughter as a single mother, "Don't ever speak badly of her father. He is a part of her identity, and she will feel these words are also about her." So we have to be aware of how we speak and treat our baby mamas or baby fathers, because it affects our children. There is a lot of healing that needs to happen in this area, especially if there were abuses that have come from our mother or father. Understanding our parents' lives and learning their history of how they grew up and were treated can help. That is why it's important for parents to talk to their children and help them to understand them, not to make excuses but just so they can somewhat try to understand us. It's this understanding that can bring awareness and compassion for our parents, so we can find forgiveness for their behaviours.

When we are hurting inside, we can become hurtful or mean. When we become this way, we begin to dislike ourselves, and we will have low self-esteem or low self-love. We cannot run from ourselves and our thoughts, feelings, and actions. That is why we go crazy or start using drugs, alcohol, food, cards, sex, shopping, etc., any addiction because we are trying to run from ourselves. We don't like how we are feeling, so we try to do something that is fun or positive, and the usual convenient source available is an unhealthy one, or so it seems. Many people only know what their parents and siblings chose to escape their sad or angry times, which is usually alcohol or drugs. What many people need to learn is the healthy way to have fun and change our mood.

If we don't communicate our feelings, problems, thoughts, and needs, how can we get help with changing them to a positive? Even if we communicate them, if the people around us are dealing with their own problems in a negative way, how can we expect them to be helpful? That's the problem for many people today. For myself, my mother or father didn't drink alcohol or do drugs, and so I only knew life as a sober person. So my parents were helpful to me in dealing with my emotions and learning to have fun in a healthy way or being able to talk with them. I consider myself lucky and blessed for this healthy start in life. This is important as parents. We need to be the teachers of healthy fun to our children, and we need to play with them. We can play baseball or lacrosse or some other game, but have fun. Laughter is medicine for the family. But this laughter must be healthy too, not at the expense of others.

The strange thing is that I was never formally educated about counselling or social work in a college or university; it came from my life and the spirits that talked with me about people and life. These are the understandings that they gave me through dreams and daily experiences. Many people weren't given skills, advice, or examples of how to have healthy relationships with themselves or others. So this knowledge has become a mystery and a void and very difficult for many to learn and maintain. Just like the woman in the jail cell who didn't have a clue of how to relate to herself and others in a positive way, we isolate ourselves from others. We give up on having a meaningful, long-term relationship. I know that is why there are so many divorces and failed relationships, which usually leads to addictions to numb and avoid the hurt or sad feelings. No one wants to feel like a failure, dumb or abnormal. We question, "Why can't I have a healthy meaningful, long-term relationship like others?" "What is wrong with me? There must be something truly wrong with me or something horribly wrong with men or women!"

But that's so true to a certain extent, because there are no classrooms to learn about yourself and others. It is a knowledge that has been lost with the whole process of learning and the unhealthy attitudes and behaviour toward each other that have made it difficult to maintain a healthy relationship. The knowledge of getting to know oneself has been lost with evolution and moving away from the ancestors' ways of living. When a people are dependent on each other and it's about survival, and you spend twenty-four hours a day and seven days a week with someone, you will get to know each other. You will want to understand and want them to understand you. You will also have plenty of time to get to know your own needs, but you were all too busy these days to spend this kind of time with each other and yourselves. When we were mean and unhelpful, uncaring to others and ourselves, we would have been talked to so that we could function and be helpful in the family or community. Today we aren't as dependent on each other, and we only spend a certain limited amount of time together. The majority of the time that we do spend with people is usually our coworkers or other students in a classroom. These environments don't really allow us to get to know each other, because we are expected to be quiet and focus on reading or writing or on our work. Our time is not to be "wasted" talking with others, not focused on our learning subject.

My people used to go fasting to reconnect to themselves and nature and the Creator to put ourselves in check with your destiny.

This fasting made you look at yourself and change the behaviour or attitude that was not helpful for you in your way of doing life.

The funny thing is we can't ever get away from ourselves, not even in our drunken times. We are still the ones left with the aftermath of our drunken or drugged-out experiences. Sometimes it isn't until we hit the lowest times of our lives that we realize what we are doing to ourselves. It's all because no one ever gives us straight-up answers about how to live with ourselves. Many times it's only in riddles, like you can't love others until you love yourself or whatever makes you happy — no one really explains enough to us, plain, simple, and clear, well, here is my attempt at it, from what I've learned from my short time here on earth, and I hope it helps you find peace of mind.

POINTER FINGER: Represents the Creator, and the part in between this finger and your thumb represents the "Birth Path." From the Creator we come from the eastern direction to the earth, and we choose our parents along the way, with the help of our spirit guide. Whichever parents we choose, we have a job to teach them something, so that's why we choose them. Many people think when they have children, they are the teachers, but that's not completely the truth. Our parents are there to teach us about some things, like tying our shoes or how to get dressed. But children are the teachers about morals and values, spiritual teachers to our parents. Children come to us to teach us about patience, acceptance, tolerance, forgiveness, and unconditional love. Parents can also be the teacher to their children if they are healthy parents, but there are no guarantees.

We are both teacher and student to each other and to our siblings. We come to the entire family and community for a good reason; we can choose to make our families proud or ashamed and disappointed. It's up to us to find that path of purpose to the Creator and stay on it. We do have the choice to go off that path for a time, but if we go too long, we can become lost and forget why we are here. We won't know what our purpose is and how we are meant to do this job for the Creator, unless we go deep within ourselves and listen to our inner voice. So it's not a coincidence, the people and family we are born into. It's all planned out by the Creator and agreed upon by ourselves.

This is probably one of the most important relationships a person can have: their relationship with their higher power or Creator/God or whatever name you may use for this source. Some have beliefs about this powerful being that put fear in them. From my experience of the Creator, this being is the opposite of fear. It is a strong force of love, peace, acceptance, understanding, patience, gentleness, kindness, love, and harmony. Everything that is good within us comes from this source.

When things happen in our lives that bring sadness, pain, anger, and disappointments, this is the one who is given the blame. Blaming him for all the negative events in our lives is a big problem for a person's faith. Our faith will start to be tested about our beliefs around who the Creator is and if a higher power exists.

The conflict with the Creator begins in our lives when things don't go the way we want. When someone hurts us, mentally, emotionally, physically, and spiritually, we tend to blame the Creator. We start to doubt if he is there and if he loves us. What people don't understand is that the harm one causes to another is not his doing. Creator just tries to bring some light into a dark situation, but we can't see out of our pain and darkness. There are people who are not listening to the Creator and have stopped listening for a long time.

I will share a personal story of a time when I was very angry at the Creator. My boyfriend died in a car accident. He was only twenty-two years old and a very innocent, gentle, and kind man. He had never drunk alcohol or used drugs a day in his life. He wanted to be able to leave no bad marks on his life path, he said. One day he was driving to the dentist, and he hit black ice on a bend and went off the road. The car went into the deep ditch, and he hit his temple against the metal part that holds the front windshield and died instantly. I went to the hospital, and the nurse told me he didn't make it. I went into shock, and my mind and entire body became instantly heavy. I began to sob. I asked if I could go see him, and she said no, because there was no one there to support me. I cried even harder. My entire body was shaking, and that was when the light went out of my vision, it seemed. I literally saw a dark veil come over me, and I could no longer see the brightness of the day, and I could no longer hear the birds singing, and no other sounds. Everything seemed unreal, and I was thinking maybe this is a dream and it's not reality.

But then my family members got there, and we were allowed into the room. Then I had to accept it when I saw his lifeless body lying there. I was so sad. That was when my anger came, and the darkness got darker. The light was put right out. I couldn't think. I don't know how I walked, I was so lost, then my younger brother got there and took me aside, shook me, and said, "Sister, you have to accept this. Do you remember Mom and Dad telling us that we are all here only for a certain amount of time, and no one knows how long that is? We are here only as long as we agreed to be here, we all have a job to do, and when we're done here, we get to leave here. You must accept it was his time and his job is done here, or you will never be okay."

That was when the sunlight burst through this darkness that had gone over me. I could see the sun again, and I could function. It was that quick. I recalled this teaching, and I accepted it. The short time I was in that darkness gave me a little insight into how it feels to get stuck there. It was a very lonely, cold, sad place that I never want to visit again. I was out of the darkness, but I still had some days and hours where I was mad at the Creator; as time went on it slowly went away. The more I realized that it was a blessing to have had an experience of being loved and knowing someone who was so awesome was a gift. Even though he was taken from me, I realized he earned the right to leave when he did. I forgave the Creator for taking him and realized he had actually blessed me with being able to spend time with him. I saw the whole incident differently when I forgave the Creator, and this is where I hear many people getting stuck. Getting stuck in the anger toward him for their pain they suffered only brings prolonged suffering.

I was told the Creator has so much love for us that he just tries his best to help us see the good in everyone and everything. But when we are hurt, we will struggle to see, hear, think, and feel the love. It's our own effort to want to see the love and goodness through our consequences that we start to understand and accept the love. To have a peaceful relationship with the Creator is to be able to accept that he knows more than us, and he is trying his best to guide and teach us all to be good people. We will all have consequences based on whatever we are thinking and acting, and it's out of love that he teaches us. It's quite the amazing thing, this gift of life. Life can be exciting, sad, happy, crazy, chaotic, fun, and loving, so many different emotions that we get to experience. It can also be shocking, sad, angering, frustrating, disappointing, and hurtful, but everything is temporary. When we learn to stop taking ourselves, other people, and everything else so seriously, we will start to enjoy ourselves. If we stop taking ourselves and situations so seriously that we miss out on enjoyment of this gift of life, we will see what a gift it is.

This relationship is so important because he is the reason we are here; it's to do something for him within our family, the people... life. I have had many moments when I pulled him very close to me because I was scared, weak, sick, or worried. But also when I was happy, grateful, amazed, and so thankful. When I see the beauty in this world, like an awesome sunset, or birds flying, a moose standing in a pond, a wolf running beside the road, all of these sights are beautiful gifts that I just have to acknowledge to the Creator for allowing me to see his amazing creations.

When I'm concerned about an individual, I have learned to pray and leave it on the Creator's desk or plate or agenda and let him get to it. If we don't believe there is a higher power that is in control, we will be very confused and can feel very vulnerable. This higher power, which I choose to call the Creator, is like a parent to me who loves me and wants to help me to succeed at whatever I chose. I talk to him everyday, and I thank him for everything that he has done for all of life. My mother taught me this: as soon as you see daylight, give thanks to the Creator for all that he has given you.

Many times people focus on what they don't have and are sad and angry with him for what they don't have, instead of looking at what they do have. I have counselled many people who haven't stopped to realize that they do have a lot to be thankful for. When we stop to acknowledge this and be thankful, it will help us to be more positive.

When we ask for guidance from him to learn the things that he wants us to or send people in our path to teach us things he wants us to know and experience, then life will get even more interesting. So this is one of the primary relationships we all need. He is the one who helps to guide us and teach us the things that he wants us to know, to be able to do the job we are meant to do here. In any healthy relationship, there always has to be a give and take. A healthy relationship is a reciprocating relationship; you must give something to get something. This is something that many Native people still practice. Some people give cloth and tobacco, some give certain foods and a ceremony; some give themselves during a fast. They will give up food and water and conveniences for four days or dance in a sun dance or rain dance.

Today people just want to take and take and take until there is no more to take or no more to give. That is what I have seen in my work. Sometimes a person will come along and make up for the ones who don't know how to give. A generous person is like a gift from heaven, but if they are over-giving or don't know when to say "I can't afford to give anymore," or know their own limits, it can be unhealthy too. Everything must be done in balance, and if we do anything in excess, it's not a good way to go through life.

My people give tobacco, food, songs, dance, a ceremony, or a gift when we are asking for help in any way, spiritually or medicinally. Medicine is anything that helps you to feel better; it can be words, advice, plants, or physical healing or a ceremony. But for many people, because of money, we think we can just buy our services and never stop to think about our genuine appreciation for this help.

I was told by a wise medicine woman, "You know we can go fast and make time for the Creator to come to us, or he can make us sick and make us listen that way. It's up to us. This is why our people would go fast; it's easier to go fast and prepare to suffer than to have it put upon us, especially when we don't expect it." This is why I encourage people to go fast at least once in their lives, or even once a year. It is good for the wholeness of a human being.

MIDDLE FINGER: Represents our family we are born into, brothers, sisters, aunties, uncles, grandparents, and cousins. The space in between these two fingers is a stage in life, on the other side of the index finger, closest to our thumb that represents our infancy. We are still very close to the Creator, and the side toward the middle finger represents our youth. We are starting to have relationships with our family and find out how we fit into this family as a youth or a child. The other side of our middle finger represents our teenage stage. Our siblings are our first teachers about tolerance, understanding, compassion, acceptance, and loving another person, even if they don't act like you or think like you, but they kind of look like you.

Being the seventh born out of eight, I got to see many different ways of handling life situations. My three older brothers and three older sisters were great teachers to me. I learned a lot about many situations from sibling rivalry, friendships, marriage, raising children, becoming independent, growing up. The lessons I got are something that no movie, book, or university could've taught; it just unfolded right before my eyes. It still does to this day, and for this I'm so appreciative being born in the place in the order I was. Each of my siblings was very different in their own way, but still lovable people.

Growing up in a small house had pros and cons. I believe there were more pros to it, but being one of the younger ones, I think I was more taken care of than being a caregiver. I mean, I did love and care for my family, but not to the same extent as my older siblings. There were four younger and four older ones, so my mother assigned one older sibling to one younger sibling, and that was how we were taken care of. For instance, my caregiver was one of my older brothers, and he was responsible for fixing my hair and making sure I had a clean face and hands, clean clothes, brushed my teeth, etc. This created closer bonds between each paired sibling; I loved my brother for all he did for me. Sometimes he wasn't as patient or gentle as my mother, but he at least tried. He still helps me today in his own way when I ask.

Another positive thing about growing up in a small house with many siblings is that I always had companionship. We always had each other to visit with, and I don't ever remember being alone. This taught me at a young age how to visit and converse with someone. My mother usually greeted us every morning with a smile and, "Good morning, how was your sleep?" It was so important as a child to see their parent smiling and happy to be awake at such early mornings. It was such a nice way to wake up, or if it wasn't her, it was one of my siblings. In our tiny room, we had two sets of bunk beds, one for the girls and one for the boys. So even when going to bed, we had each other to visit as we were drifting to sleep; I loved that. All of this closeness taught us that if the atmosphere was peaceful, then we had a great visit. Our house was too small to be angry with each other; it made the day go slow if we were mad at someone. So I learned to apologize quickly and to try to be as cooperative, helpful, and respectful as possible. These skills have helped me to have some great times with people.

Some of the negativity in our small house was that someone's needs were not always being met. We couldn't possibly get all our needs met. There were too many of us, so we had to learn to compromise and accept that reality. Some might see this as a negative, but in reality it helped me in many relationships. I accepted that there were others in this world, and sometimes it's okay not to be so demanding that things to go your way. You will be much happier to learn to go along to get along. As siblings you might sometimes assume that you are all alike, possessing the same values, perspective on life, parents, and siblings, but no two people are the same. Even identical twins have different personalities, values, likes, and dislikes, and so this is the way people are. In many families there are conflicts because we assume our siblings will act like us, but this is where we are mistaken. When we expect our family to uphold our unique individually made values, beliefs, and ethics, we set ourselves up to be disappointed, hurt, then angry.

I counsel many people, and so many times I hear of the different conflicts that happen between siblings. These strained relationships develop because people keep doing this to each other. If people want to have peaceful relationships with their family members, they must accept that their siblings are not the same people as them. They will have difficult relationships if they keep expecting a certain behaviour. We have no control of anyone's actions and thoughts, only our own. We must accept that our siblings might have grown up in the same house, with the same parents, but this doesn't mean they will be just like us. We can learn to celebrate the uniqueness and enjoy the differences or be constantly disappointed and angry with them for not acting the way we want them to. This is called control issues, when we aren't happy unless people are behaving as we want them to. It might seem silly when we really take an honest look at ourselves wanting to control everyone in our lives. The only way some people can do this is through instilling fear in others through threats, but that only lasts so long. Eventually, fear no longer works, and there goes the control. Then we will try different emotions to try to manipulate another person, pity, love, and anger, just to name a few.

In my childhood, we spent a great deal of time outside playing. My father made lacrosse sticks, and so we would play that game a lot. He didn't make them to sell; he made them to teach my brothers how to make them, and also so we could play. But sometimes these lacrosse games could turn ugly. If someone took the game too seriously or if someone got hurt or if someone had to be the goalie, then there would be a conflict. We knew if we fought over this kind of stuff, we would be told to put away the sticks. So, many times we would just go with the flow and work things out. This is a skill I've learned from a young age: accept that you might not always get what you want, and that's okay. Maybe the next day you will get what you want because you compromised the day before. This is how I would see the situation; I would say to myself, "Okay, maybe I can't get what I want today, for sure tomorrow or the next." I will remind them about fairness and how I didn't get my way the day before. This is a skill my mother taught us: be fair. If you got what you wanted this time, keep that in mind and let others have their turn. Eventually, everyone will get what they need, then people can be happy and feel equal and that fairness was given.

My parents never treated any of us any different than the others. They never said, "I love you more than her or him." There was no favouritism, so I learned from a young age that I was equal to everyone, even the older ones or bigger ones. This taught me that I was important and valued, no matter my size or age, so I should therefore value everyone, no matter their age, size, and so on.. We all had different needs, and they tried to meet those needs. For me, growing up and seeing how busy my parents were working and raising us, I never really wanted to bother them with my needs. It wasn't that I felt insignificant or unworthy; I just loved my parents so much that I never wanted to overwork them. If I could do something myself, I would. If I could solve a problem or conflict myself, I would. It made me happy not to be too much work for them.

One memory that stands out was when I got into the fight with an older sister. I mean, we had disagreements in the past, but this one was different. I was fifteen and taller and heavier than my older sister, but she was bossy and wanted to tell me what to do a lot. I think she thought that was how to be an older sister. One day I refused her demand, and she freaked out on me, we got into a wrestling match, and I got her into a headlock and held her. That drove her crazy, and she was threatening many kinds of harm to me, but I kept talking to her to try to calm her down. It felt like I was holding on to a wild animal that was going to attack me if I let her go, maybe even rip up the whole house. My other sister came into the room because I was calling out to her; she thought I was the provoker. She started yelling at me to let my other sister go. I told her the situation as I was holding on to my angry sister. I remember thinking, *Sometimes I guess I will have to stand my own ground, and if it comes to being physical to protect myself, I can, but I don't want to get physical.* I felt very powerful, but at the same time I was sad and embarrassed that we had to come to such a situation that I had to make this statement. So I learned that I never wanted to get into a situation like that again. I need to learn to speak up and set my boundaries within myself and express that to the people around me so I would never be in that type of situation again. Thankfully, I never had to fight anyone in my life, though I almost did once. Again, I stopped myself because I didn't want to feel the shame and sadness.

Growing up in that crowded house, we all had wants and needs, but our mother had taught us to share. She taught us to be patient; we could wait to wash up and brush our hair. We could wait to eat; there would be enough for everyone. My mom had a rule about giving things out too: youngest first, then next youngest, and so on. She told us to always take care of the youngest ones first because they were so small; no one would see them and they'd be ignored. She was always kind of extreme in her stories of why we had to do things her way, but there was still some truth to what she was saying.

A very important start to my life was the fact that my siblings respected my parents and each other. I'm not sure if we had ever heard the word "respect," but we were taught it through my parents' rules of the house. Also in the way my parents behaved toward each other, us, and other people. I can remember my mom greeted everyone with a cheerful "Hi," or "Good morning, afternoon or evening!" She was friendly; she never talked negatively about others. My siblings were kind and caring to me, and it was a household of comfort, calmness, relaxation, and fun. We didn't necessarily always play with the neighbourhood kids; my playmates were mostly my sisters and younger brother. We made mud pies a lot, it seemed like everyday, but it couldn't have been because it would get cold and snowy.

I think that was the best lesson I learned with my siblings growing up: cooperation. Everyone can help out some way and not to be pushy or bossy about how you're going to help out — just help in some way. I know everyone has had different experiences with childhood, and some had jealousy, abuses, fighting, sibling rivalries, etc. I have experienced this with my two older siblings. They were always competing to be the "boss" when my parents weren't home. If they left my sister in control, my brother would get mad trying to assert his power over her. This would get out of control sometimes, but I was never scared because it was between those two, and we younger ones just minded our own business and played or watched TV. We had learned that they would have an argument, and it would be settled.

My parents were very much a part of solving our conflicts or disagreements; we were never left to figure out our problems ourselves, until we were older, of course. But even then, they helped us if we asked. There were boundaries that were clearly defined in our home about how we were to treat each other. This is an issue I see that can make relationships very difficult with siblings. The boundaries with material things were murky because we had to share everything, but it was clear that we were the only one responsible for our bodies. Two sisters and myself wore the same size clothes, and also my brothers wore the same size clothes, shoes, etc., for a while. Well, actually, my parents taught us that our body belongs to the Creator and it is only loaned to us, so we're supposed to take care of it and return it to the Creator just as we received it. The biggest lessons I got from growing up this way was to accept others as being different. Not everyone is going to want or like what you do, and that's okay. Accept that fact that no two people are the same, not even siblings. This doesn't mean we have to be enemies or fight about it. We can accept it and keep going about our day. But if we treat one another, especially siblings, with love and respect, we will always have someone in our corner who trusts us and cares for us, no matter what, hopefully.

THE RING FINGER: This represents our community. What we learn in our homes translates into how we treat other people. How we think and understand others is demonstrated through our treatment of them, especially as a child. We learn as we grow how to fit in our community, especially when we become parents. The way we have treated others throughout our childhood and youth is remembered and is either dealt with in some way, or our children will hear how we were as a child or a youth. We have to be careful and taught always to keep this in mind: what we do we will answer for to our children. It's important to know that people don't forget, and we need to made aware of this as we are growing up, to be able to be accountable for our actions, even as children and young people. This is how chiefs and clan mothers and faith-keepers were chosen in our communities; their actions and attitudes really tell who a person is.

Sometimes, when we go through death or difficult situations, it can challenge our beliefs about each other. This story was a real situation that I dealt with regarding two sisters' love being challenged. These two sisters were best friends for many years until the day their mother died. Their mother had left the house and land to one of the sisters, but not to the other. These two sisters had always lived together with their mother; the one sister who got nothing didn't understand why her mother would do this, and she was very hurt. The other sister didn't really think this was a big deal. She was the younger one and actually was the baby of the family. Only for the sake of telling this story will I give her a fictional name of Alice, and her older sister's name was Lucy.

So Alice figured the land and house was left in her name because she was younger but still elderly; she was in her mid sixties and would probably outlive Lucy, who was almost seventy-one. Lucy had a different thought; she thought that her mother always spoiled Alice and loved her more than her. This was not true, but Lucy truly believed it. So about six months after the death of their mother, this thought had bothered Lucy to the point of starting to mistreat Alice, which she never did before all of this. When Alice came to see me she, was so devastated, because Lucy was planning to move out and get an apartment because the relationship had become strained. Alice felt that she had not only lost her mother, but she had also lost this best friend, her older sister. She wanted advice on how to fix this problem; they were almost at the point of not talking anymore.

There were other siblings in the family, but no other siblings were fighting that way, and they didn't want to get in the middle of the problem. So Alice was so lost without the companionship of her sister. After a few sessions with her, I advised her to try to sit down with her sister and tell her how she felt. Alice was afraid that Lucy wouldn't listen or believe her. She knew that her sister couldn't really afford to move out, but she didn't want to stop her because she was afraid that Lucy would just leave anyway. I explained to her that maybe she thought she knew her sister and that she didn't really know what was going on inside Alice's mind. She had to accept that she didn't know what Lucy's thoughts were, and she was obviously hurt. If she wanted to preserve this relationship, she needed to have a difficult discussion and ask her why she was treating her that way. She must tell her how she felt and ask her to reconsider how she was thinking about all of this.

Alice knew that her mother loved Lucy just as much. One of her maternal aunties had told Alice the whole reason her mother left the house and land to her was because Alice was younger; she trusted her to let her sister live there with her until she grew old and take care of her until then. So, during one of our sessions, I asked her to try bring her sister to our next session to come fix or heal this relationship. Her reply was no, she didn't think she would come, and Alice was afraid of being rejected and more arguments with Lucy. This is what happens to many relationships; we become traumatized by the meanness that we experience in other's behaviour, and we don't want it to happen again, so we give up and don't try.

Eventually, over a few more sessions she realized that it was necessary for her sister to come to have this difficult conversation. We were able to get her into the session because I asked Alice an important question: "Is this relationship worth more to you than being rejected?" The difficult conversation happened, and we got to the root problem, getting them to hear each other's truth with the thought of the LOVE always present. They resolved their differences through a very emotional dialogue in which we heard the hurt from Lucy at being left nothing by her mother, but with the explanation shared by Alice that it was the most logical solution.

Alice explained how she never wanted to live alone at the house that all three always shared. When Alice shared what their auntie had told her about why their mother left it to Alice, Lucy felt better and realized Alice was very innocent in the whole situation. Alice had not influenced her mother; Alice didn't know anything about her will. They both agreed they loved each other's companionship and wanted to live in the homestead and continue helping each other. Lucy stayed living with Alice, and they became best friends again. There were some apologies and some honest conversations necessary, but everything was mended. Neither sister had children; they only had each other in reality to consider family. It was their long relationship and their memories of all the good treatment they had to remember to dispel the recent negative thoughts. This is the importance of treating people well, especially our family. This is what can happen when two people really want to mend a misunderstanding. If only one of them wants to mend the relationship and the other person doesn't, then it won't get mended. It takes both to mend a relationship; we can apologize and do our part of taking responsibility, but if the other person doesn't want you in their life anymore, it won't happen.

As I have travelled about and met many people, I have learned that not everyone has grown up this way. Their homes might have had alcohol, drugs, violence, abuse, neglect, competition, favouritism, and unhealthy parents, siblings, grandparents, cousins, aunties, and uncles. I first dreamed when I was a teenager about these types of households. In the dream, I was in a Native community, and I was staying in a very nice house, but it was cold in there. I had my children with me, three daughters, so we had to sleep together in one bed to stay warm. The first night I slept in that community, I dreamed I was taken to a house where there was a party. At this party everyone was drinking, and there were children there who were trying to stay to the very outside of the room, along the wall. The children seemed very scared, then an old man started to call one of them to come sit with him. The boy was saying no, no, not me, no, Grandpa, not me this time!! The other children were trying hard to hide and were very scared and pitied this little boy who was only five or six years old. Then the old man grabbed him by the arm and said, "Grandson, you're coming with me!" He dragged this little boy crying and screaming down the hallway to a bedroom, and no one noticed because they were all drinking and talking. I knew that this old man was molesting his grandson in the bedroom, but there was nothing I could do as a spirit looking in. Then this woman's voice said to me, "This is what Grandpa means to them. Not everyone has had a healthy family, and this is what you will have to deal with here." Then I woke up.

The next day, some people from this community came to me and asked me to go see a boy who was acting out in class. As I walked into this counselling room at this school, I saw it was the same boy from my dream. I started to talk with him about family and how family can become our monsters. His eyes opened wide, and he started to listen. As we talked back and forth for two to three hours, he shared with me the abuses that he was experiencing. In the end he wanted to move to another home, but the fear of this happening at another home was there. He didn't trust people anymore and believed that one day this old man, called "Grandpa," would die anyway. He did have some good experiences of his family life, and that was what he was holding on to.

The message I gave to the boy was, "Your spirit is about goodness. We're always wanting good behaviour, whether it's from yourself or from others, and that's good. When we have these healthy expectations for unhealthy people, we set ourselves up to be disappointed, hurt, then angry. We do this most to our close family members. Most people are unhealthy, and some are really unhealthy with a lot of addictions and abusive behaviour, whereas some people might gossip or be antisocial and not try to have relationships at all. So you must accept that your family is unhealthy and expect unhealthy behaviour. Your grandfather needs help to understand the damage he has done, as well as the damage that has been done to him; this is what he needs to heal. There are many people in your family that need this kind of help, but you can only do healing for yourself. Is this what you want?"

His reply was so innocent and loving through his tears. "I just want a loving and happy family. Can't we help them all?"

I said, "Only if they want it."

He accepted my answer, and then I asked him if I could go talk to his family, and he said, "Yup, 'cause if you don't, things will never change for us, right?" I said that was right.

During this dialogue, I realized I had a choice. I could be silent to the principal and school counsellor and let them continue to label him as a troubled child, or I could say something to the family. I asked to go to speak to the family at their house; the school counsellor took me there. As I walked up to the house, it was the exact house from my dream. I was a bit scared, but I knew I had to be courageous for the sake of the children of this house. Once inside, I saw the remains of a drinking, party-house, empty beer bottles lying here and there, but they allowed us inside. I met the mother and father and a few other teenage siblings who weren't at school but just getting up. It was around noon by this time, and the school counsellor insisted on accompanying me to hear what I had to say. She seemed very uncomfortable in this home because of the dilapidated conditions.

So she started to explain who I was, a traditional healer who had come to the community to help with some difficult situations. Then I started to speak. "I need to speak to the grandfather, is he here?"

This was the paternal grandfather; the father was defensive and asked why in a loud, angry voice. I said he was part of the problem of the son's behavioural problems, as well as the parents.

He became even more defensive and asked, "What do you know about this household and family? Has my son been telling his lies again?"

I replied, "He has told me enough about abuses to have police brought here, but mostly I was shown in a dream what the problem is here, and unfortunately your son confirmed this."

The father and mother got a scared look on their faces, and the teenagers slunk back into their bedrooms. It was apparent that the grandfather and the father's unhealthy behaviour were affecting the whole family. I stayed calm and continued to speak. "I need to talk to him or I can talk to him at the police station. Either way, I will get my chance to talk to him, so we can try to do this as respectfully as we can, or we can be aggressive about this problem here."

The mother came closer to me and asked what her son had shared. I said, "I will tell you after the conversation with your father-in-law." So she went in the bedroom where he stayed and got him. As he walked down the hall, I could tell by his walk that he was ashamed and afraid. He sat down in his chair very heavily, plopping into it. He wouldn't really look into my eyes, but I didn't care. I told him who I was and how I had a three-hour conversation with his grandson about abuses going on in the house. He kept his head down as I talked. I told him, "You are the problem of this young boy. I know what you did to him and the other children in this family and neighbourhood. You can leave and go to the police station and turn yourself in and see what becomes of you, or you can wait for the police to come arrest you. Your grandson just wants you to get help. He doesn't want to send you to jail, but that's not up to him. Somewhere still inside your loving grandson, he believes you have goodness inside you, and he wants you to get rid of your demons, or the garbage that makes you do the harm to him and your other victims."

This man had been taken to a church-run residential school, and there he was molested by priests and nuns. His life was good until he was five years old and stolen from a Native village as he was out with some older siblings hunting. The abuse started the day after he arrived at this school and continued until he was fourteen, when he ran away. This was his story that he eventually was able to share with his family. Of course, this was some time after his stay at a healing centre and dealing with all the garbage of his life story. He was finally able to tell his story without fear and shame.

This is a typical story that I have heard many times. You can switch it from a boy to a girl being molested, but the molesting is usually from a family member; it's not usually a stranger. This is the sad reality and outcome of residential/boarding schools that were run by a religious denominational church. Many of these Native children who survived these schools came back to their communities and brought this unhealthy behaviour back home to their family. So all this hurt, rage, frustration, and disappointment that has been continuing into present day, this is what is causing the abuse of alcohol, drugs, suicides, self-harm, rapes, and murders. The statistics of all these social ills in Native communities are off the charts, but there aren't many details about the lack of help that these communities receive. The governments in many countries where Indigenous people have been affected in this way have tried to suppress this information. The only news Native communities get in mainstream society is about all the negative behaviour from this impact of colonization.

The family that was affected by this one incident went on to get the help they needed through the healing centres and through ceremonies. The peace that was restored to some of these family members once the healing began has brought sobriety to this family. This is just one story where peace was restored, by this one brave, little boy who just wanted a loving, healthy, and happy family.

When we are hurting inside, we have choices about how to deal with it. Unfortunately, it is usually addictions that many people choose because it is more work to face yourself and find courage to speak your truth. But like the little boy in the story, there is much to think about with the topic of jail, courts, lawyers, etc. There are many people who don't want this for their family members who are unhealthy; they just want them to get help. These are the complicated thoughts that go through the mind of a victim who has been abused by a family member. This distracted thought is what preoccupies the minds of many children and adults, replaying these traumatic events and triggering those same emotions. This is a person who is not at peace with their life events; this is the cause of many mental illnesses. This is where many people are at when it comes to these types of situations. and this is a majority of what I hear. I mostly deal with adults; only some are children when they are brought to see me. I ask them what they mostly want. By this point they have moved out and have their own family, but the abuse haunts them.

This is what they are asking for: "How can I just be okay and not let this bother me anymore?" "How can I live without anger, rage, hate, and fear from this experience?" "I don't want to carry this hate anymore!" "I don't want to mess up my kids because of this event that has happened to me. I'm not sure how to be a healthy parent."

Then I usually ask, "Do you want to have peaceful thoughts about this person and your childhood?"

"Yes" is usually the answer. There aren't many people who enjoy being miserable and angry; they just learned that this way of being is a protective way to be. We carry these emotions because we are afraid if we don't stay angry or keep talking about this, it will happen again or they will get away with it. Usually people will talk about these abuses when they are drinking, so they can pretend not to remember the conversation and blame it on being drunk. They will come to a point where they are sick of this haunting them and causing them to continue to abuse themselves. Over time, being angry and miserable will take its toll on your own quality of life. Your mental well-being is usually stuck in a negative place, focusing on the negatives. This is where many lose their faith in a higher power; they have said to me, "Where was God or the Creator when I needed him?" I tell them I can't answer that, but I do know that no one gets away with anything they do. There is always a consequence for their actions, and sometimes we will see this happen or hear of something horrible happening to them. Mostly, I've see that it will come through sickness that they will have to deal with these demons of hurting others. The guilt that many people carry when we have intentionally hurt others is punishing enough, and this is another reason why many use alcohol or drugs, trying to escape these emotions. Siblings are our first teachers about fairness, cooperation, fun, playing, and caring for another human being, if they are healthy. If they are unhealthy, those who experience abuse from siblings are still suffering from their childhood trauma. Everyone acts from what they have learned or experienced, so it's hard to blame just one person. I have learned that human beings just want to be able to dump their actions on someone else; many don't want to take responsibility for their actions, so they blame. But this doesn't resolve their anger or hurt; this just leaves a person feeling justified in their anger, so they're still not enjoying life. It comes from the spiritual need to be loved, cared for, safe, nurtured, and valued. When these needs aren't met, our spirit is the one who is hurt and saddened. Our body has memory of trauma as well; it's called body memory. A person will have reactions that might be extreme because of the body memories. So even if we try to push these memories away, we have a spirit that remembers, and our body remembers.

Parents are our first teachers, they give direction for our family to travel down a path, but every person must eventually choose their own path. Many times as parents we pressure our children into a life that we want for them, but if this isn't their destiny or their want, we can't make them walk down this path.

Since many Native children were taken into boarding or residential schools and abused and traumatized, when they returned home to start families, they had horrible examples of how to treat children and each other. This effect on the children took many of the healthy parenting skills from them when they became parents. The knowledge base was limited; the only good things that they were taught were sewing, cooking oatmeal, cleaning on their knees, and some farming skills. Mostly, the impact was very negative: starvation, extreme discipline, and sexual, mental, emotional, physical, spiritual abuses. These parents did the best they could do considering what they were given; the harshness of these experiences never leave a person healthy. I applaud all those who survived this horrifying experience, and their children who had to survive the abuses that they brought into those families and communities.

This is the struggle that I have heard so much with children who had abusive parents or controlling parents. They say, "I know I should love my mother or father, but for the horror that I experienced during my childhood, I can't forgive them." Sometimes their parents aren't alive anymore, but they still talk about them like they are. This anger is what makes people physically sick and denies them a happy and healthy life.

When it comes to community, this is usually an aspect of feeling a part of a larger population. The word "community" speaks about a group of people coming together in "unity." So many people have lost the idea of unity, and how do we become unified? This is significant question that we need to ask ourselves: "How am I contributing to the unification of this collective group of people?" Here's another good question: "What's my attitude toward others in my community?" "Do I feel a part of this community? If not, why not?" "Have I tried to become a part of this community?"

These are some of the important questions we need to ask ourselves when it comes to how well we are relating to our community members. It's the same with our family; we must not put healthy expectations on unhealthy people — and most people are unhealthy to a degree or another. Accept this fact about unhealthiness and ask yourself, "What can I expect from unhealthy people? Unhealthy behaviour." When we stop expecting healthy behaviour from others, we will stop being disappointed, hurt, then angry. We are the one who makes ourselves angry, and we are the ones who can make ourselves happy as well. It's when we realize our true power with our thoughts and attitudes that we realize how wonderful life can be; if we continue to expect people to change, we might be gravely disappointed, hurt, then angry.

To help with your relationships within families, have patience with each other. Cooperate with others. It makes life more peaceful and the job easier. Accept others; no two people are alike, not even siblings. This can be a blessing; life would be boring if everyone thought the same. Give others an opportunity to do things their way, and you will be able to have your turn to do things your way. Take turns going first. Communication is vital in any relationship. We must be able to communicate our needs, values, and thoughts in a respectful way, but don't expect others to be the same as you. Just because you're siblings, don't assume you will think the same way, or have the same values; every person is an individual with independent thoughts. Accept this fact and you will be able to get along better. Enjoy the differences between you and your siblings; celebrate them. Life and families would be boring if everyone were the same. Here is a thought you can carry if the differences between you are so far apart that you cannot have them be a part of your life: "I love him/her, but I don't like their choices of behaviour." To love someone doesn't necessarily mean you need to see him or her everyday or have them physically close to you. You can love someone from a distance. Learn to forgive on a daily basis, if not hourly. Children can forgive five minutes after an incident, learn from them, as they are very new to being a human being, they are mostly spirit.

Our friendships are usually are most peaceful ones because these people are a choice we make to have in our lives, unlike family. However, for that reason it is sometimes difficult to have peace always present in these relationships. It is more difficult because we see these people as comfortable and fun. We don't have as many expectations of them as we do of family. They're not usually someone who causes you grief. However, when they do behave in ways that aren't acceptable or have opinions you don't agree with, you can see them differently, or vice versa. When we behave in ways that our friends don't agree with, this can cause problems.

The best friends I ever had were the ones who didn't judge me or have a strong opinion about what I was doing. They chose to give their strong opinions when they thought I was overstepping boundaries. That was when I knew they cared enough to say what they felt was serious enough to express. I must say, my best friends were my sisters and my younger brother. They were always present when we had a visit and needed to talk growing up. Today we are all grown and have our own homes, families, and lives, but we still try to make time to visit each other.

The relationship with friends or coworkers is that they usually start to become closer, sometimes more than family. Since we spend so much time with them and share conversations about our lives, we can become close. It's these relationships that can be sometimes the hardest to deal with when we have a conflict or disagreement, because we don't expect it.

When conflict happens in these relationships, we must ask ourselves once again, how important is our relationship with this person?

THE PINKY FINGER: Represents the ancestors. Our ancestors are the decedents of our families that have died. We believe their spirit leaves the earth and goes onto the spirit world in the heavens. This place is past the stars and is a heavenly place where we get to go to when were done our work here on earth. We all come here to do an important job for the Creator and when we're done this task, then were done here and we get to die. Our body goes into the ground to help to continue life here and the spirit leaves this earth plane. Our ancestors still care about us and are able to help us here on earth. We have to learn to talk with our ancestors or relatives that are in the spirit world.

The side of this finger closest to the ring finger represents the grandparent stage. We start to think about our ancestors who have passed away, or our relatives that we grew up with. We become focused on what we accomplished in our lives and what difference we made here in our time on the earth. But at any time, you can touch your pinky finger to your thumb. What that means is you can be close to the ancestors at anytime in your life and ask for guidance from them. It doesn't only have to be when you get old. When you can close your hand and make a fist with your thumb on the outside holding the rest of the fingers, that is when you have mastered all these relationships. But until you can do this, you need to be able to hold your thumb within them. This represents that you must learn to love yourself before you can love anyone else. You need to look at what makes you up, your mother and your father. So you need to be able to love your mother and your father, to be able to forgive them for however they treated you and love them. The way you forgive them is to look for something that is good about them and find love for them for that goodness. Then you can love yourself.

If you can't love yourself, start making choices you're proud of. This begins in your thoughts, which lead to your feelings, which lead to how you act or behave. Another way to find love for yourself is to appreciate the difficulties you've experienced and acknowledge the strength of yourself for surviving your obstacles that you have had overcome. This is how to appreciate and love yourself. Finding love for yourself is important because when you can look at yourself and love everything about yourself, good and bad, then you will be able to do the same for others. When we live in denial that we have a negative quality, we not living with truth. We need to look at all parts of ourselves and embrace all that we know is there. The good qualities, and the bad or negative qualities need embracing too. It's like having twins inside of you; one is mischievous, rebellious, mean, deceitful, a cheater, quitter, a gossiper etc., and then there is also a good side. This twin is the good one, or the one who we like more and like to embrace more. This side of us is sharing, caring, kind, helpful, a good listener, and all those nice things about us. This is the side we want people to acknowledge and notice the most and appreciate. But when we don't honestly acknowledge the negative qualities in ourselves, we become angry and judgmental about others that allow that side of them to show. This is when we won't like other people and these qualities that they show to others, because we are trying so hard to suppress this part of us. It's like we are angry, jealous, or envious of people who allow that twin out to play. When we accept, embrace, and love our negative side, then we can love and embrace others for their negative side.

Teachings of the Good Message

T HERE WAS A MAN WHO lived among my people in the 1700s, a Seneca chief named Skanyadiyoh (Beautiful Lake). He didn't make the best of choices while he was on the earth, so the story is told. He drank alcohol too often and didn't treat his family well. When he was old, he became sick and went into a coma. Our people of that time didn't quite understand a coma, only that he was near death and in a deep sleep. His daughter took care of him and fed him and kept him with her and her family in her house. For four years he was in a coma, and every now and again he would mumble or talk in his sleep. Finally, one day he woke up and slowly became stronger physically, and he started to share the visions that he had while in the coma. These are some of the teachings that he shared...

Many people stay in relationships that aren't healthy, and they think it is for the better. Or they tell themselves it's for the children, or it's a family's expectations that when a person gets married, it's for life. If they get married through the church, they tell them for better or for worse, and that it's for life. Even if it is unhealthy and there is plenty of meanness, abuse, and fighting, they are expected to stay together. He was told by grandfather spirits that the Creator doesn't want us to be with a person if we're mean to each other. If, when you wake in the morning, the first thing you do is argue, until you go to bed at night, it's not good to stay together. If a couple argues and fights a lot, this is causing damage to yourself, your children, and the other person, and this is wrong in the eyes of the Creator; you shouldn't be together. We are instructed to try to work out our differences. We should be nice to each other, not get jealous of each other if we are spending too much time with the children. Not to listen to gossip — this can cause problems too.

Another teaching he gave is to not to get involved in your children's fights. He said, "Children will forgive the other child and be friends with them the next day, but the parents will not." Children can forgive easier and quicker, and it will cause problems in the families or community. The adults won't talk for years because they don't know how to forgive as easily as children.

When it comes to children, he said we need to listen to them because they have wisdom too. We shouldn't think just because they are young they don't know anything; there is wisdom in everyone. Another teaching he gave was not to gossip about the father of children. Don't say that a baby's father is not his or her father and that it looks like a certain person other than their father. This is bad in the eyes of the Creator.

Another teaching he gave is that when a man beats up his woman or his children, his consequence will be when he dies he will spend eternity beating up a burning steel figure, and pain will be throughout his hands, feet, and legs if he kicks people.

These parts of our body are given to us to show love; as women we may do this by cooking, cleaning, bathing our children, hugs, working, anything that shows we care about people. Men can hunt, work, help around the house, hug, bathe their children, lift heavy things, help their spouse. Use your health and body in a positive way, and you will stay healthy.

Another teaching he gave is that these grandfathers showed him what happens to people when they have alcohol in their lives. They showed him an area and told him to look and tell them what he saw. He saw two groups of people. One group was eating, and everyone was happy and laughing and being nice to each other. Then he saw another group of people that were drinking alcohol, and women were getting raped and beaten, and men were fighting each other, and women were fighting each other. People were killing each other, and the children were crying and there was no food. Then the spirits told him, *Tell the people to not drink alcohol (the rotten juices of food); if they do this, they will live this and see these things. The Creator wants them to eat the food naturally, when it is still new and healthy. Then they will have a happy and healthy family and community.*

Another teaching he gave was that the Creator wants us to share our food, especially with children. Sometimes they will come to your home, and maybe they haven't eaten in days, and they are starving. Feed the children; don't be stingy with your food. When you feed them, you do a great thing for the Creator, because he loves all children. When you do wrong to children, you do a great wrong.

Also, don't be stingy with your food with your neighbours, if you have enough share with them; someday you might need this help. We never know what our neighbours are living through.

Also, among the women, if you're visiting another woman, sweep her floors or do her dishes. Help her with her housework. When you go there to visit, don't just take from her; give back to her also, and she will appreciate this.

In your community or village, don't go around telling lies or gossip about another relationship. Don't tell a woman, "Your man is with another woman in another community," or a man, "When you go away to work or hunt, your wife is with this other man." When you tell lies and gossip, this hurts a family and can cause it to break apart. This is a great wrong to the Creator, because the children will suffer.

These are just some of the teachings that he gave to my people a very long time ago, and we still remind our people every year. We have speakers who have trained to remember his story and to tell his story so that our people will know how the Creator wants us to be.

A male elder in my community once told me about how his father had taught him about being married or having a family. His father told him, "If you want your wife to grow old with you gracefully and healthy, help her with the hard work around the house. Don't let her lift heavy things, then she will stay youthful and healthy. Think about how you are going to be helpful the next day; this is what you must think about before you go to bed at night. How to be a good partner, sister, mother, father, daughter, friend, grandmother, grandfather. Then you will have a plan for the next day. Don't just think about yourself and your needs."

A teaching my mother gave me was, "If you be nice to your partner and he is nice back, then it will be a good relationship and you will have a great life with him. But if you are nice to him and he isn't nice back, then it won't be." It is very simple but true, and it goes both ways. I have seen women take advantage of kind, healthy men too.

Many times we wish our relationships to be good, healthy, and happy, but it takes two to have a healthy relationship. If one of the partners doesn't believe that is possible, or they are incapable of being nice, you won't have a happy and healthy relationship until the both or you want this. That's the importance of finding a suitable person in this world; because of this freedom of choice, we get to decide how we will act toward other people. It is especially true when you start to have a family, because this is when the real tests begin about how you feel about people. Our issues will show in our relationships with our partner and our children; the way we treat them is what we really think of men or women. For instance, if we have sons and we are very mean or abusive to them, whether it is emotionally, sexually, or physically, it comes from the belief that was created by our own experiences of our childhood. If our father or uncle or brothers or grandfather was mean to us, then we might believe that all men are mean, and therefore we can be mean to them. Our actions tell our true feelings of our hurts or our respect and gratitude to our father or our mother.

This is the hardship of parenting. Sometimes, becoming a parent happens early in life, and we haven't began to deal with our pain or our issues with our childhood. When we are hurt by others when we are children, that affects us for a long time, and it creates beliefs. These beliefs will show in our actions. So if a man beats a woman, this says that he didn't like the way his mother or grandmother, aunties, and sisters behaved. It also tells us that this man is insecure with himself and the relationship. Sometimes he beats women because he wants to scare them into never leaving him, no matter how badly he treats her or the children. Sometimes it's due to his frustration with the relationship. He hasn't learned that if only he was loving, caring, helpful, and nurturing, they wouldn't want to leave him. He is maybe acting out of what he saw from his father or grandfather of how to be a man, husband, uncle, father, friend, or boyfriend. We are designed that way.

We will learn by what we see the most of, and some will learn from what they heard, and some will decide how they will act based on their own experiences. For instance, some men grow up with an abusive father, and they see him hit his mother and maybe himself too, but he decides he will never hit his wife or children because of the pain he lived. So it is very individual how we will choose to behave. Some people might use that as an excuse to say *I'm like this because of my father or my mother was*, but it's still just an excuse because they can choose to be different. I had a boyfriend who lived with many different kinds of abuse and dysfunctional behaviours with his siblings and parents, but he decided he wouldn't act the way that these people did that hurt him or disappointed him. Instead, he decided he would be the opposite.

He taught me that it can be an excuse that people would use to misbehave or to mistreat others. Everyone gets to decide how they will be as a person. That is the gift that the Creator gives us:

we decide how we will be. If we have good examples of how to be, then we know what it looks like and feels like to be around nice and kind people. If we have angry, mean, or selfish people around us as examples of how to be, we can decide also if we want to be this way or to be different.

The Learning Process

W E THINK THE LEARNING PROCESS only happens in a classroom. That isn't true; we don't have a learning process that helps us to get to know ourselves or understand others. Our education system becomes focused only on facts, knowledge, and logic about everything except our thoughts, feelings, body, and spirit. Unless we make it to university and we study psychology or human behaviour, only then will we kind of understand people, and even then that research can be wrong. We want to be accepted, understood, and forgiven, not judged. This is our greatest wish, yet how willing are we to give this to other people?

Seven Grandfathers

I want to share a story of the seven grandfathers; it is a story that I hold very dear. The story tells how to treat other people and how to see the love and power that we all possess. My maternal grandfather was Chippewa or Anishnabe and this is a story that explains many teachings and also how the sweat lodge came to our people.

A very long time ago, when there were only Native people living on North America (Turtle Island), the people became very sick and weak. It seemed like if they simply fell down or if they caught a simple cold, they would die. One day, a young boy about the age of ten years old went to the elderly men in the village and asked them, "Why are our people so weak and feeble? Why does it seem like it doesn't take much and our people can die?"

The elderly men replied, "That's a good question. Why don't you go up onto that hill and fast and ask the Great Spirit these questions."

The young boy said, "I will." Then he walked toward the hill in the distance. The elderly men tried to stop him; they told him they were only joking, and he was too young to go fasting. He didn't care. He told them if this was the way to find the answer, then that was what he would do. The elderly men couldn't talk him out of going fasting, so they decided to help him. They prepared him for what he might experience, and they lent him a bear hide and gave him medicine and tobacco. They told him to make a tobacco tie and pray to the Creator to ask for the answer of how to make the people stronger. So they put him up on the hill toward sunset and told him not to be afraid and to try to remember whatever came to him. The first night he went out to fast on top the hill, he floated up into the dark sky. He was afraid in the darkness, then slowly he could see there were seven grandfathers sitting in a semicircle in front of him. Each grandfather had a white light behind him as he sat in this darkness. The grandfathers talked to him; they each had a teaching for him of what would help strengthen the people — what was missing with the people and why they became sick.

1) **HUMILITY:** This is represented by the wolf. The wolf lived for his pack and the ultimate shame is to be outcast. Humility is to know that you are a sacred part of creation. Life life selflessly and not selfishly. Respect your place and carry your pride with your people and praise the accomplishments of all. Do not become arrogant and self-important. Find balance in within yourself and all living things. The wolf came in a dream to me one time to teach me humility. In the dream I was walking

2) **BRAVERY**: This is represented by the Bear

The next grandfather talked about bravery. The mother bear has the courage and strength to face her fears and challenges while protecting her young. The bear also shows us how to live a balanced life with rest, survival and play. To face life with courage is to know bravery. Find your inner strength to face the difficulties of life and the courage to be yourself. Defend what you believe in and what is right for your community, family and self. Make positive choices and have conviction in your decisions. Face your fears to allow yourself to live your life.

3) **HONESTY:** Represented by either the Raven or the Sabe

The both understand who they are and how to walk in their life. "Sabe reminds us to be ourselves and not someone we are not. An honest person is said to walk tall like Kichi-Sabe... Big foot, like Kitchi-Sabe, Raven accepts himself and knows how to use his gift. He does not seek the power, speed or beauty of others. He uses what he has been given to survive and thrive. So must you. The seven sacred teachings of White Buffalo Calf Woman, say to walk through life with integrity is to know honesty. Be honest with yourself. Recognize and accept who you are. Accept and use the gifts you have been given. Do not seek to deceive yourself or others.

4) **WISDOM**- Represented by the beaver. The beaver represents wisdom because he uses his natural gift wisely for his survival. The beaver also alters his environment in an environmentally friendly and sustainable way for the benefit of his family. To cherish knowledge is to know wisdom. Use your inherent gifts wisely and live your life by them. Recognize your differences and those of others in a kind and respectful way. Continuously observe the

life of all things around you. Listen with clarity and a sound mind. Respect your own limitations and those of all of your surroundings. Allow yourself to learn and live by your wisdom.

5) **TRUTH:** Represented by the turtle: Truth is represented by the turtle as she was here during the creation of Earth and carries the teachings of life on her back. The turtle lives life in a slow and meticulous manner because she understands the importance of both the journey and the destination. Truth is to know all of these things. Apply faith and trust in your teachings. Show honour and sincerity in all that you say and do. Understand your place in this life and apply that understanding in the way that you walk. Be true to yourself and all other things.

6) **RESPECT:** Represented by the buffalo. The buffalo gives every part of his being to sustain the human way of living, not because he is of less value, but because he respects the balance and needs of others. To honour all creation is to have respect. Live honourably in the teachings and in your actions towards all things. Do not waste and be mindful of the balance of all living things. Share and give away what you do not need. Treat others the way you would like to be treated. Do not be hurtful to yourself or others.

7) **LOVE:** Represented by the eagle because he has the strength to carry all the teachings. The eagle has the ability to fly highest and closest to the creator and also has the sight to see all the ways of being from great distances. The Eagle's teaching of love can be found in the core of all teachings, therefore an eagle feather is considered the highest honour and a sacred gift. To know love is to know peace. View your inner-self from the perspective of all teachings. This is to know love and to love yourself truly. Then you will be at peace with yourself, the balance of life, all things and also with the creator.

When the little boy was brought back to earth to tell the people what we were lacking to make us stronger, he couldn't remember everything. He started to cry and say that he would fail the Creator because he can't remember everything. He heard one of the grandfather's voice telling him to stand up and turn around. At first he was facing east to watch the rising sun, he turned to the west and his shadow was pointing to the west and at the end of the shadow was a lodge. Inside this lodge he saw the little white lights and the there were seven of them and they instructed him to bring the people inside there and they would be in there to help to strengthen the people. That how the sweat lodge came to the people, and that's what its for. So when we get hurt in life and could become angry or afraid, we can go into this spirit lodge and they would help our spirit to be renewed and this goodness can come back into us. By goodness, I mean our teachings of being a loving and respectful and all those teachings from the grandfathers. The spirit of those seven grandfathers would help us to shed our anger and hurt so we can be whole again and a good person. This was given to us to allow us to come back to being more healthy in society and in our family.

COMMUNICATION

The art of communication in any relationship is necessary and important, no relationship will last without it. Using our voice and our words is the only way we can transmit what we are thinking and feeling, however actions speak louder than words. Our actions really tell our true thoughts, attitudes and beliefs we have about self and others. Many people are given the message as a child to be seen but not heard. Therefore there have been many people who don't know how to communicate too well and this is what makes relationships very difficult. There is more messaging in our body language than actual words expressed. Our facial expressions and our presence is a message in itself without even using words. Our tone of our voice is a big expression of putting our emotions into what we are trying to transmit to others. The art of diplomacy is something that my ancestors were known for. We can say what we need to in the most respectful way possible, however because of the traumatic events in our history with the colonization process, there has been much more anger expressed. This is why the main stream media likes to depict Native people as being so angry, war-like people, however, we don't worship war like the Europeans, Canadian and United States governments. They are forever doing parades and doing special events to honour war veterans. We value people who are more capable of settling differences with negotiations or meetings and conversations. This is where many mainstream people talk about the peace-pipe, smoking the pipe and discussing difficult topics was necessary. The tobacco used was different for different nations but my people use a tobacco that is grown for thousands of years. When the pipe is used, the spirit world, our ancestors, the Creator were all asked to listen and be a witness and help with the discussion. So in essence, we were making an agreement in front of the Creator and the natural world were all witnesses to our agreements. This is why Native people never used paper or contracts to document our agreements, it was all with the pipe or tobacco and this was more meaningful. We believed that this way was the best way because if agreements were broken, the universe would do the correcting or give the consequences. A broken agreement was highly frowned upon, our teaching is that you're only as good as your word.

This is one of the biggest differences between men and women. When a little girl is growing up, she is never told not to be too gentle, or emotional, or sensitive. As little girls, we are allowed to be as nurturing, and this is done when we are given dolls and we practice being a nurturing person from a young age. As we start school, the friends we choose are very influential as to what is acceptable behaviour. If our friends are healthy and open with their emotions and respectful, we won't feel the need to guard ourselves, especially our emotions. We can be just as emotional and deep with our conversations as we want. No one ever tells us to stop being a little girl if we cry or are emotional, sensitive, gentle, or nurturing.

However, as a little boy grows and enters the school environment, he is faced with other little boys. This is when a little boy starts to learn that if he is too emotional or too sensitive or too gentle, he will be teased, laughed at, bullied, or called a girl! This becomes his first lesson, to put up a boundary of being able to show only a certain amount of emotions. Each individual, depending on how healthy or unhealthy his/her environment is, establishes a boundary. As this little boy grows, it starts to become very clear to him that he can't show his emotions so openly, or he will be teased.

This is all fine how life is going, and the boys are hanging with the boys and the girls are hanging out with the girls, but we all know that this usually changes. When we become young men and young women, we usually start to be interested in the opposite sex. When we start a relationship with the opposite sex is when we start to experience many new emotions. One of the biggest obstacles when we have a relationship is understanding each other, and the only way we can do that is through communication.

However, the way we have learned to communicate is very different from each other. When little boys have an argument or disagreement, if it is a strong issue, it usually will turn into a fistfight or a wrestling match. Usually it is more about establishing the alpha male, or the dominant male in the school ground or classroom. So, eventually, men learn not to take issues too personally or too seriously; they choose their fights wisely. They learn this because of the physical fighting nature of boys. If a man grows up to be the alpha male, he usually learns that bullying or being physical with the person questioning him is the way to deal with that person. This is why people can grow up physically, but not spiritually, mentally, or emotionally. To grow mentally and emotionally is to look at the experiences one has and learning to change attitudes and beliefs that are immature. Being physical with someone is a very immature way of handling a conflict. Many may disagree and see that being physical is necessary at times in life; however, it is the wisdom that has shown me that there is always a more respectful way to handle a conflict.

Now, as a female, we have all these great deep conversations with our girlfriends as we are growing up and into our teenage stage, then we meet a young man, and we want the same kind of conversations and relationships that we had with our girlfriends. We want them to share their emotions, be sensitive; we want deep conversations and totally open up as we have with our girlfriends. Then the horror starts. Most young men will not respond as we would like. These men seem, cold, insensitive, unemotional, maybe even uncaring to our needs, or so we think. But this is not entirely true. Men do have emotions and feel; they have just learned not to show it the way that women do. It's very frustrating and hurtful to us inexperienced young women. It's just as frustrating and difficult as young men, because he does care about the relationship, but he has learned how not to show his emotions, and now the LOVE OF HIS LIFE relationship depends on his ability to express these emotions. This frustration and disappointment does not end, as many of us know who have tried to have a relationship many times. It's kind of funny when you really look at boys and girls and then men and women. They grow in opposite directions; the woman grows more emotional and open, and the man grows more closed, if they are in a healthy environment as they are growing. However, I have met men who were in an opposite position, raised in a very loving environment with grandmothers and female relatives who loved and protected them. They meet a woman who was raised in an unhealthy environment, and she was the one who was closed, cold, and unemotional.

What I have come to believe is that every couple is put together to teach each other about being healthy and unhealthy and the frustration that each one feels with their situation. The awareness and behaviour we choose is always based on our unique, individual experiences. My teaching from a spirit, if you want to see the healthiness of a man, is you need to look at the healthiness of his mother. If a man's mother is healthy (emotionally, mentally, spiritually, physically), then he will have a healthy attitude toward women. If a woman's father is healthy (emotionally, mentally, spiritually, physically), then she will have a healthy attitude toward men.

One of the biggest problems as women within a relationship is we are always wanting and trying to have the same kind of relationship that we had with our girlfriends with our boyfriend or husband. This is the same with men; they want their girlfriend not to talk so much, or not to talk about such emotional, deep, serious topics. I counsel many men, and they have said to me, "Why do women have to talk so much?" "Why can't they just say what they have to and leave it?" "Why do they have to go on and on about an issue?" "I wish they would just tell me the problem and suggest a solution that's simple, let's hear the problem and discuss solution."

Many men learn how to pretend to listen to their wife or girlfriend to fool their partner into thinking they are concerned and listening. I laugh when I see this happen, and it is very often, especially at a shopping mall or restaurant. When women notice this glazed look in their husband's eyes and he's not really present, they should just stop talking. You are only wasting your breath at this point. Let your husband take a break to digest the first hour of your conversation or vice versa. From a man's point of view, a woman who goes on and on about the subject only wants to hear herself talk. One man said to me, "I swear my wife has impossible expectations from me with her ability to talk and me to pay attention and answer her pressurized questions and expect an answer very quick."

From a woman's point of view, "My husband never listens to me. I can tell he shuts his ears off or something just when I need him to listen to our problems. He just doesn't seem to care." Or "My partner never talks to me. He's so quiet, it worries me 'cause he never shares his feelings with me." "It's so frustrating trying to talk to him 'cause he just doesn't want to discuss anything."

These are some of the things I have heard in my counselling sessions. The strange thing is sometimes a couple can be together twenty or thirty years, and they still don't learn about the differences in how we communicate. My husband once said to me, "If I don't say anything, we're good (meaning our relationship), when I do say something, that's when I might have a misunderstanding or a problem understanding your logic or behaviour." So the message he gave me was, no news is good news. I had to learn how to accept my husband and his lack of communication needs as perfectly fine. The deep conversations I had to learn to have with my mother, sisters, girlfriends, and female coworkers. My father once said to me, "Stop trying to make your husband into a woman. Men don't behave the same as a women. You think he is unemotional or uncaring, but he's acting the way a typical man acts. He cares, he just don't show it as easily and openly as a woman."

As women we need to learn not to go on and on when we're upset. The best option is just to say what we need to and then leave it for them to think about what was stated. If we keep talking, we overload them; it's like a classroom. If a teacher goes on and on without giving the students time to digest and process, they become tired and overloaded with information. That's why most men dread the words, "We need to talk." It usually means, "I got something to say, I'm upset, and you're going to listen to me. Even if I talk all night, you better stay awake and pay attention." But imagine you're in a classroom with a teacher talking physics or biology and it just goes on and on and on. That's what it's like to have to listen to a woman, from a man's point of view.

When I've been counselling men, they have said, "She never wants to talk about cars or motors or fishing. These are some of subjects that I'm interested in, and she never wants to talk about these subjects. She only wants to talk about our problems and her feelings." Many women wonder why their partner prefers to hang out with his buddies. Let's look at some of the reasons why they would. Most males have expressed how their male friends accept them just as they are. Their male friends do not have any deep conversations with them or have high expectations of them when they hang with them. They can be as laid-back, lazy, and gross as they want, and their friends don't yell at them or have hours of discussion about how they behaved badly, unlike their wife or girlfriend. The conversations are very light, unemotional, but interesting for other men. If there is a problem in the relationship or behaviour, they address it and it's done, nothing that goes on half the night in a conversation (while they're very tired).

I find it funny how much we don't know about each other, as men and women. When I explain to men how a woman would hear certain sentences and how a man would hear explanations, it is so fun to see the clarity that comes to people. Sometimes I still make mistakes with my husband about the clarity of what I'm trying to say to him.

Siblings

I have counselled many people in their difficulties with their siblings and not speaking to them anymore or the breakdown of their relationship. The feelings get kind of cloudy in these relationships, because the parents don't make it clear as to how they should relate once they have grown up. I try so hard to teach my daughters as I was taught by my parents. It's not always easy to have healthy, close relationships as we would like, but it can be somewhat healthy if we make an effort to make those relationships significant in our lives.

People need to stop reacting when it comes to the people that are most important to them. So many times I hear how this brother isn't talking to this brother or sister anymore. I ask those people who are coming to me for advice or counselling, "Is this person important to you? Does this relationship mean very much to you?" If you answer "yes," then you need to make an effort to do everything to try to make it "work." The reasons are you don't want any regrets when you look back at your life choices. Making it work means something different for everyone involved, so that needs to be made clear. A conversation needs to happen to discuss whatever the issue is, and then the solution needs to be discussed and negotiated. The art of conversation has been lost, so here are some ground rules whenever you're trying to resolve a conflict: 1) Only one person speaks at one time; 2) mutual respect with your choice of words; and 3) taking turns to express feelings, and these expressions need to actually be feelings or emotions, not just statements with "I feel..." at the beginning. An emotion or feeling is something that can be expressed with a facial expression, for example, "I feel disrespected." This states, "I think based on how you act or speak towards me that I don't feel you respect me." Then the response might be an argument, because the other person may feel like they do, and it might not be true. How do you show "disrespected" with a facial expression? The feeling actually is "hurt, sad, angry... etc." but we don't realize this emotion. It's this kind of communication that causes so much breaking of relationships.

Another sad moment with siblings is when we realize our brother or sister has changed and become someone we don't know. Many times it's the abuse or the pain they try to cover up with the abuse of alcohol or drugs that develop that person's character, and they don't behave the same as we knew them. Men and women develop differently, emotionally, mentally, spiritually, and physically. It's true in most cases that women mature earlier then men; the reason I say in most cases is because that's not always true. The development of emotions is a difficult part of the human being because it's not as acceptable for men to be emotional. But I've met women who weren't allowed or encouraged to be emotionally healthy either. When a person isn't allowed to express and be free with their emotions, or it's not a safe environment to share feelings, they don't develop healthy expressions of emotions. When a person is encouraged to and not ridiculed or shamed when they express their emotions, they are free to share their feelings.

A good male friend of mine who was fairly healthy complained to me one day, "My girlfriend doesn't talk much. She's cold and is not very emotional or nurturing."

I told him, "I've heard this a lot with women complaining about men this way, but this is the first time I've heard of a man wanting a more emotional woman. When I met her, I thought she was very cautious but didn't find her too cold. Then, as I spent more time with her, I noticed that she was not a very touchy-feel kind of a person. So I asked her why she wasn't very emotional or touchy and nurturing. This was her answer: "I wasn't treated with much kindness and gentleness. When I shared my feelings I was ridiculed or they used my pain to hurt me more, so I stopped sharing my feelings."

Then I told her, "Your boyfriend is in need of more nurturing and gentleness, and I'm sure he won't hurt you if you share your emotions more often." She told me that she knew that and it hurt her because she couldn't understand herself why she was that way. I told her how we are very habitual people, our responses become habitual, and all she needed to do was think about how she would like to respond and start to respond in a way she would be proud of. They eventually married and have a family now. I saw her again a few years later, and she told me that what I did for her helped her to find her heart again and not be afraid of expressing her love and vulnerability to the right people in her life.

There are some relationships that can't be mended due to it taking both people to want to have a better, healthier relationship. This is the heartbreak that I have experienced too, siblings, couples, friendships, family members, neighbours not getting along, but one of the parties wants to have a better relationship. It takes two to have a relationship, and if both parties are not willing to work on their own attitudes and behaviour, then it can't happen. Most relationships are broken to due to "Healthy expectations for unhealthy people." We put these healthy expectations on the people closest to us, and then when they don't behave the way we want, we get disappointed, hurt, then angry. No one signs contracts with us to say they will behave a certain way if they are our parents, aunties, uncles, cousins, partners, siblings, friends, boyfriends/girlfriends, best friends, coworkers, or neighbours, yet we expect them to behave a certain way, and when they don't we're mad, and we begin our manipulating ways to get what we want or think we deserve. When you really want to take an honest look at yourself in a relationship, ask yourself, "Am I trying to manipulate the situation/person to control or get what I want from this person?" Then ask yourself, "How would I feel if they were behaving this way to me? Would I like me?" or "Would I like it if they acted this way with me?"

Acceptance

Acceptance is the key word of relief, when we learn to accept our person we are trying to have a relationship with for all that they are. And if we still like to have this person in our lives, we must learn to accept them as they are and stop trying to manipulate them into changing and becoming the person we want them to be. This will only make them unhappy; they can only act a certain way to be accepted in our life — is this fair? If the person you are trying to have a healthy relationship with is unhealthy, and to a degree that you can't handle or accept, then move on. Let this person go and let them be themselves and you be yourself. However, if this relationship is valuable to you, then you need to evaluate the person and ask yourself, "Are there more positive qualities about this person than negative?" "Is it more my attitudes and behaviour that are causing war between us?" "What am I contributing to this relationship? Support? Acceptance? Love? Encouragement? Compliments? Help? Respect? Positive attitude and behaviour, or am I the person adding to the unhealthiness of this relationship by behaving badly with manipulative thoughts and actions?"

This is why it takes two to have a good relationship; we can only change ourselves, not others. If only one of us is looking at our-self and changing our self, then we might be able to maintain and cope within a relationship and actually be happy. But we can't expect the relationship to be a really great one if the other party is not doing their work. In order for our relationship to get better, we have to have the other party willing and ever diligent to accept their flaws and get help or become their own self-reflectors/mirrors of themselves in an honest way and change it. Since we are habitual people, it takes time for us to change a reaction that has served us in the past. Maybe with our parents or siblings, when we were children was when we learned certain behaviours that served us then, but as we age those manipulating behaviours will no longer serve us as adults. This is the awareness of immaturity of our thoughts, emotions, and actions when our relationships are not working out.

The three main manipulating emotions are, pity, love, and fear. Some of the statements you might have heard before sound like this, "If you love me you will do this…" or "I will kill myself if you leave me or if you don't do this for me…" "I don't have any money or place to stay, so I need to stay here with you, no one loves me, etc."

These statements are used when a person is manipulating a situation, and although it may be true or not, is it fair or healthy for that person to hold another person emotionally hostage at any time? No, these people are not healthy mentally or emotionally, because they are unaware or uncaring of another human being's feeling and needs; it is only about themselves and what they need. A person should never want to have a person in their lives if it is causing another person such pain and unhappiness. It is time to let go and set the person be free to do whatever makes them happy. Otherwise, both will become unhappy maybe resentful and bitter and feel like they don't have a choice.

Life is given to us for two main reasons: freedom of choice and happiness. So we get to have the freedom to choose whoever and whatever is in our lives that makes us happy. Don't get me wrong — it's not that person's job to make you happy. It's your job. But if this person's personality, values, compassion, and so forth are what attracted you, then it should be easy to be happy with someone like this. However, if they lack helpfulness or caring, then this maybe an upsetting factor. It is all up to you; no one can tell you when you're happy. Everyone must get to know themselves well enough to know when this is the right person. Many times we lose ourselves in the relationship and put our own needs so far away that we forget what we want or need to be happy. Or sometimes people will leave a relationship because they are unhappy, but if they have children, the children aren't happy. Parents sometimes forget or don't realize that their happiness is dependent on the children being happy. People need to stop and really know themselves before making decisions. Never ever make a decision when you're upset or emotional; it almost always is not a good choice. When we're emotional and we act or make a decision, it is an emotional one, not a well thought-out, wise decision. This is when we usually have regrets and are ashamed or embarrassed with our actions and chosen words. We actually hurt ourselves because of hasty, quick, emotional decisions, and we hurt the people we really love and care about. But they have hurt us in some way too, and this is how we justify our choice of behaviour, even if it is a choice we don't really want. Teenagers are well known for this kind of behaviour; this is the heartache and heartbreaks for them, because they are so emotional due to the hormones. These hormones. affect our emotions and this is why we are so extreme with happiness, sadness, joy, anger, etc. This is usually such a terrible time for us human beings, we lose friendships, boyfriends, all these different relationships are so important to us at this time. I think if a person gets through their teenage years without have a heartbreak or an ending to a friendship, they are very fortunate, cause this is usually the time this happens. The reason is we are just really learning how to value another person. We are just learning how we feel about ourselves. This is a learning time to discover our own likes and dislikes, our own values and morals. We start to break away from our family or group mentality and start to come into our own thoughts and attitudes towards life and others.

All My Relations: We Are All Related

THIS STATEMENT IS A POWERFUL belief that the Indigenous people share about all of creation, including all peoples and our environment. We believe that the earth is our mother, and everything that has life is our relative, including the sun, moon, thunders, stars, plants, animals, birds, trees — everything. That this is our first family is the belief of many Indigenous people, and this is the foundation of our values. Because of the relationship of the people and all of life being family, we know there is a responsibility to take care of this relationship. If we want a healthy relationship and mutual respect and care, then we have to be responsible for the well-being of "all of life."

When the hunters take an animal for their family, it is necessary for many Indigenous peoples to offer tobacco; in the north I know the Inuit offer water into the mouth of some aquatic animals. In any case, there is an offering and a prayer for that animal and gratitude for giving up their life for the survival of their family. Even when medicine people go to pick plants for herbal cures, they offer a prayer with tobacco, asking the plant to help the people who need it. In any case, as Indigenous people we have traditions that have been passed down from generation to generation to honour and respect all of life. Unfortunately, along with the European invasion came an attack on this knowledge and relationship with nature.

So there are some Native people who don't use this knowledge and way of having a relationship with our relatives.

When it comes to people, there have been many influences that have affected our knowledge and traditions of the rules of how to treat each other. Here are some of the traditional teachings that I have had the pleasure of learning from my own parents, siblings, and children, as well as many different Indigenous peoples I have visited. One of the best messages that my mother gave me was, "You are never above another human being or below them. You are equal, remember that." This was her exact message to me: you're just as important as anyone, no matter who they are. Not even a president, principal, queen, or judge are above you; they are only human, as you are. They don't have anything more unique or special than anyone else. Every living being is special; the Creator has made everyone, and he loves everyone the same. Treat them this way. You don't have the right to mistreat or think of anyone as less than or below you.

So when we look at the disagreements and conflicts that have happened in the world, there is always one side that believes itself to be better than, smarter than, or more privileged than the other. The spirit within everyone has a need to be at peace with others and self, and if we carry the attitude of being the only correct one and have closed thinking, we are not at peace. Conflict is really an opportunity to find out what others think; they may have a very good idea or knowledge that you don't have. You will never find this out if you have a closed mind and judge and label the person or group. We need to open our hearts to each other and be willing to listen to others when we have disagreements. There is growth that happens to people when they are able to open their mind and hearts to listening to a different knowledge or perspective.

Gossiping is a big part of creating unhealthy attitudes toward others, and it teaches our family that it's acceptable. But this act is actually a big negative tool for disharmony within families, communities, and organizations. Many wars were created this way, through gossip, rumours, propaganda etc., making some people or races of people into villains. Many people think gossiping is not that bad, but it's one of the bases for war. So the next time you go to repeat or start gossip or rumour about someone, this is an act of war. You are starting a conflict with that person. Doesn't that make it seem that much worse than minimizing it as just gossip? It's a sneaky way of hurting someone or a family or an organization. Then I've heard the question, "But is it still bad if it's true?" I believe it's always about intentions; you must think about the intentions behind why you're spreading the rumour or continuing the gossip. Is it to inform for a good purpose? Do you know is this rumour is 100% true? Is it helpful to you to repeat this? How is this information helpful to you or others? These are just some of the questions you must ask yourself when you hear information and if you think about repeating it.

Another obstacle is the unwillingness to want to have a peaceful relationship. Sometimes when we think we have tried long enough to make our relationship better and it doesn't work this way, we stop trying. We work hard to avoid people so that we can stop feeling frustrated and hopeless. It's our frustration that we don't like feeling because we can't change or control others. We have put conditions on our relationships: I will accept and be happy with this relationship if they act like this or think like me. With these conditions we might never be happy or at peace with them or very many people. We essentially believe that we are right and everyone else is wrong. Is this reality? I don't think so. If we continue to think this way, we will disconnect with everyone, because at some point we will disagree with everyone. If our attitude is that we are smarter than everyone else or we have a right to not be challenged, we will find it difficult to have a relationship. For instance, many times parents will think this way, and when raising their children they won't listen to their thoughts, ideas, etc., because they are the parent. As the parent, they might think they are wiser or more intelligent, but this isn't always true.

Peace Building

F OR MANY YEARS I HAVE been doing different forms of peace building circles, I studied at a university to get certified as a conflict resolution facilitator. During my studies I was asked to do some leading and facilitating as many of the tools used to resolve conflict came from Native peoples' talking circles, healing circles and peace building circles. I started to first be interested during my time working in the Women's prison. The training I received was only three weeks where I shadowed a veteran Native inmate liason worker who worked in Kingston Ontario at the Prison for women, otherwise known as P4W.

The greatest tool I had going for me was the ability to remain calm in situations where many of my collegues would be panicking. During my training at P4W we had an eventful time as there was a woman being brought in who had participated and helped her partner to lure and kill innocent, young women. The women were infuriated with this woman and the idea that they had to share space with her. The atmosphere was full of anger and disgust for this person. It was difficult to have any kind of circles or discussions without her name being brought up and the women becoming infuriated and outraged. It was a tense time for everyone trying to remain calm and not increase the emotions of anger and rebelliousness. These women wanted to hurt or kill her as they mostly had daughters or nieces that were the same age as her victims. This was a time for learning for me to help the women to remain peaceful, even when I myself was disgusted and not liking this woman.

We had many circles to try to keep the women talking instead of getting physical with this person or anyone who was protecting her. We discussed how its okay and normal to feel these emotions of disgust and anger, but its not okay to act on those thoughts. We would talk about the consequences of following through with those kind of thoughts. This is the lesson that I learned at this time. We have a right to feel angry with the actions of others, but we don't have the right to bring harm onto another just because we don't like what they did. Many years ago my ancestors would banish people who didn't have a healthy behaviour toward others. If they wanted to steal or harm another person, they were confronted on their behaviour and then told to leave that village. This meant usually death to them as they needed others to survive. So this was a similar attitude that the inmates had with their population. When someone did something that was too abusive or wrong in their eyes, that person was not accepted into any group of people. They were isolated and attacked as often as they wanted to teach them lessons. So in life whenever anyone has wronged or hurt me, I would work very hard to fix my own mind and heart as to not allow that person to break me. When a person allows themselves to be broken is when they allow the harm or abuse to consume them and poison their heart. The poison is the anger and hateful thoughts. That anger is what causes so much stress and dis-ease in an individual, so to not allow the unhealthy person to permeate your loving being, you must be strong and protective of your loving self. During the circles that I have conducted, there are many stories of abuse and violence that people are capable of doing onto others, which is a reality but a sad reality. The accountability and consequences that we as an individual or as a society want as a result of being hurt is understandable, because we want to feel safe. However, were not always in the presence of the person who harmed us, so we don't get to see what's going on in their lives. Faith in the Creator and his watchful eye on everyone is a must to get anyone through this type of harm. The spirit guide of the person who does harm onto others is responsible to give out the consequences to the person. Those consequences are well thought out and are much deeper in lessons that any human being could give. This is the message I was given when it came to my own hurts and wanting to harm that person back for causing harm to a loved one. I had to return back to my loving self and allow the Creator to do the consequence to the person/people doing the harm. No one is immune from Karma or Creator and his knowledge of what a person is doing or even thinking of doing. I learned many years ago to not even think of harming or stealing or anything like that because when that actions comes back to you, it is usually much harsher than what you did.

When I have to convey this message to angry or hurt people, its not always well received. These peace building circles are for this purpose, to talk about these emotions but to also bring back to them the healthier thoughts to carry so they can have peace. Sometimes it's a meaningful apology that can heal that anger or hurt in the person. But sometimes an apology don't come from the person who caused the harm, but I try to give them an apology for them having to experience this. It's very difficult for individuals to accept that they might not ever receive the apology or changed behaviour that they want, but to forgive and bring themselves the gift of peace within is for themselves and the people around them. I truly believe that it isn't our right to punish others, but it's right to give consequences, like distancing yourself from harmful people, even if it's family. Its okay to remove people from your loving heart and place them outside of your heart to let them have their consequences without feeling guilty.

One part of dealing with family and the abuses they can bring, like sexual abuse, mental, emotional or physical abuse or any of these abuses, is the complicated feelings that the family has to deal with. Sorting through the emotions that abuse from a family member causes is like picking up a handful of dew worms. We can try to lay out each worm and name that worm as an emotion and keep doing this to be able to sort through the complicated feelings that come when family hurts family. This is the difficulty with facilitating these healing circles, there are many complex emotions and can be overwhelming. When hurt comes from a stranger or someone outside of the family, it's kinda easier to process, but unfortunately it's usually family members that hurt other family members. This has been my experience with these peace circles, so sometimes it takes a few hours to get everyone participating and sharing their feelings and thoughts around the event that caused the peace to leave us. The main element is to being successful with these circles is to establish the safe space for everyone, someone has to be the person who takes that responsibility that they will make sure everyone is feeling reassured they are safe.

The bottom line is everyone gets to decide who they will come to terms with the hurtful actions of the people, it's so true that hurt people, hurt people. Not one person can tell another how to feel or relate to another person. I have forgiven many people who have hurt me, but it doesn't mean I allow them into my space or life. It means that my mind and my heart is clear of their presence as I don't want their poisonous behaviour to ruin my outlook of life and people. There are healthy people and unhealthy people in this world, if you look at their actions, you will be able to see. During these circles we talk about all these philosophies about life and behaviour and thoughts. To bring another person back to a place of peace is a very emotional and powerful ability. It takes determination and a willingness to allow the person to gently come back to peace, but only if they want to. Some people are like the traditional chiefs from long ago before the "Peacemaker" came to us, they don't believe that we will be okay without our war clubs so some wanted to continue to hold onto those clubs. Some had to see over time the benefits to being peaceful rather that dishing out the punishment. Karma is much more creative to teach people lessons who want to harm others. She is relentless and very much in your face about showing the person the mirror. The mirror is the theory of having a person be in your presence who is like you, if you like to take advantage of others than you will have this type of person take advantage of you. Or if you are someone who is very vain, then you will be given the presence of someone who is shallow and vain as well. This is the mirror consequence, I myself believe also in the good karma affect. If you're good to others than good will come to you as well. The Creator feels the sadness, hurt and disappointment that you feel when someone takes advantage of the innocent, the vulnerable and the abusive person becomes a target of consequences.

Tools to Help with Peaceful Relationships

Forgiveness

FORGIVENESS IS FOR OUR OWN mental health, which leads to emotional and physical wellness. What is forgiveness? This was the answer I received: "It's when you want to see the goodness in that person again."

Forgiveness unties you from the event and person, letting go of any anger, revengeful, hate, or bitterness toward the person who has hurt or disappointed you, and allows you to think compassionately about them.

I will share a dream that was given to me at a time when I was very angry and sick. I dreamed I was in a canoe on the river behind where I grew up, the Grand River. There was a grandfather-spirit sitting in the front of the canoe, facing toward me. There were one inflatable boat tied on the right side of my canoe, and inside was an ex-boyfriend. The grandfather spirit said to me, "I want to talk about your anger toward this man," pointing at my ex-boyfriend. He continued, "I want you to think about forgiving him; this anger is only affecting you, not him."

It made me mad just thinking about forgiving him. There were two other boats tied to the left side of my canoe, and inside those boats were cousins. These cousins had betrayed me as well. The grandfather continued, "When you hold grudges and angry thoughts toward them, we must keep the boats tied to yours. Who is struggling here?" And it was me. I was paddling so hard so that I didn't go downstream.

He said, "They're getting a free ride with your angry thoughts. When you can stop having angry and vengeful thoughts toward them, then we can untie these boats. And who controls the current?"

I answered, "The Creator."

He said, "Right, and he has much more resources and creativity to teach them a lesson about their hurtful behaviour. If you are willing to pray for the Creator to have pity on them and wish them well, we won't ever tie their boats back to yours. You see, anger and hate weigh you down and stop you from being able to travel many places. If you can learn to forgive people everyday, it will leave you with a light boat."

I said, "Okay, I will," so he untied my ex's boat from mine, and he drifted away emotionless. It seemed easy. Then he asked if I could forgive my cousins. That was easier, so I said yes. We untied their boats, and they drifted downstream and away from me. Then my boat was very light, and I started to paddle all over the river.

He said, "If you can learn to forgive every hour, only then you can be happy. Even if you tell people how to treat you, it doesn't mean that they have to treat you this way; they still get the freedom to choose how they want to act. So when you can untie yourself from the anger and hate of events in your life that were hurtful and from the people who caused it, then you are free of this pain. If not, this pain will stop you from enjoying life."

This is the greatest skill we can ever incorporate into our daily lives. It is a way of being happy and not carrying around all the wrongs that people have done to us and we have done to ourselves. This skill is for you; it's not for the person who has harmed you. It is a way of life to be forgiving is something you must work on everyday, every hour. If we can learn to do life this way, we will learn not to carry around all this hate and anger toward anyone, including ourselves. It is not an easy skill; it takes skill to pay close attention to yourself and how you are thinking and feeling. Without learning to forgive, you won't be able to be at peace with your life, past, present, or future. When we worry ourselves sick, we are not at peace. We are in a state of fear and no faith. This is probably the worst state we can carry with us, and we cannot be happy in this state.

Ganikwiyo (a good mind): To have an awareness of your thoughts and the self discipline to change your thoughts to a good thought. A good thought is being able to look for something good or positive about the person or situation. Being able to find the lessons in the events that were difficult or hurtful is the greatest gift you can give yourself. The most painful events are the most important lessons, you have to pull the strength or awareness that you can from that experience. Regrets are only there if you didn't find the lesson learned from that decision or choice of behaviour. Mistakes are necessary for us to learn not to make that same choice again or we will have another lesson and the lessons get more difficult when we repeat the same behaviour. Having healthy expectations for unhealthy people is another way that we can not be at peace with people. When we can accept that those people are unhealthy and ask ourselves, what can we expect from an unhealthy person... unhealthy values and behaviours.

Faith in Karma: Having faith in knowing that the Creator or Karma is going to teach these people lessons when they cause harm to others. The spirit guides are the Creators helpers that teach us lessons everyday, it's very simple, bad choices bring bad consequences, just as good choices bring good consequences.

Conclusion

THERE ARE MANY SCENARIOS WE can face in our lifetime that allow us to carry hate, anger, or rage for someone. I have heard many reasons why a person feels justified in not forgiving or accepting a person or circumstances of life events. All this action does, is give the person permission to go through life unhappy and being controlled by someone's behaviour. When they no longer want to change their mood from anger, hate, or rage to peaceful, loving, or calming behaviour, it's very difficult to help them. A person must be willing to want to come to a place of peacefulness. Sometimes we must be willing to forgive the event or person, even if they are not sorry. There have been times when a person died and never apologized for their wrongs or harm that they did to others. I have had to counsel people so that they wouldn't continue to be angry for the rest of their lives. It is possible to imagine that person who did you wrong and tell their presence or spirit you no longer carry hard feelings, or hate or wish harm to them. This is what frees them from that person, and if not, the person continues to be tied to that negativity.

Being at peace with a person who is living or dead is a freedom that you gift to yourself. This takes faith that the Creator or God is the only one who is responsible for dealing with each of us and our good or bad behaviour. We come to this world mostly as a spirit and are given a body to get us through our life experiences.

As we go through life, we are meant to learn about emotions, situations, and relationships and whatever else that we experience. When we return to the spirit world, we have to tell our story of our experiences of our time here on this earth. So life isn't as critical as many people think in terms of doing everything right or perfect. Life is meant to be lived and enjoyed, even though it might not go the way you plan.

The Creator is the one who is control of our lives. We can make plans, and hopefully he gets on board with our plans, but that's not always the way it works out. To be at peace with yourself is to accept yourself with your flaws and your strengths. We need to embrace our mistakes as well as the great things we have done; it's all necessary to form us into who we are. When we do make mistakes, our mind becomes open to new ways of doing things, or at least it should become open. This is when the Creator steps into our lives to send us a new or better way of doing life. When we take the approach of life from a victim's point of view, thinking that Creator is picking on us and punishing us, we won't see what he is trying to teach us. When people harm another person, this person is not connected to their own spirit and therefore is not listening to the Creator. So when a harmful person hurts others, many times people lose faith in the Creator, but obviously they're not listening to him, since he is all about love. The harmful people are only listening to themselves and their own hurt, and this is what controls them.

People need to know this, because we all have the freedom to choose what we will do with our pain. If we want to create peace, then we need to deal with our pain and heal from it so that we don't harm others. If we harm others from our pain, we will bring pain to ourselves. What we do to others, we do to ourselves. Our spirit is always remembering what we do, because when we die, this is what continues to the spirit world to report back to Creator of our experiences here on this earth. Our spirit guides are spirits of people who lived before us and are responsible for giving us lessons and also karma. We never get away with any kind of mean behaviour; it does come back to us, and this is called bad karma. When we do good behaviour, we create good karma, and this also comes back to us. This is how we must think and conduct ourselves in order to have peaceful relationships. It takes faith and understanding that there is more to this world than you think. There is a spiritual presence in our daily lives, and many people have lost these understandings and teachings. This is what has caused so much mean behaviour from humans to others and also to creation. Our environment is full of life, and those things are also our relations. When we are abusive to the earth or any form of life, we are also creating our own suffering. We must try to have a peaceful and loving relationship with our environment as well. Our Mother Earth is suffering because of many greedy, needy, and selfish people. All of life is connected, and we will all suffer if we don't make peace with our mother the earth and all of creation, which includes us.